AF473753

LIVING PAPER

LIVING PAPER

First printing of the first edition, January 2020

EDITED & PUBLISHED BY SendPoints Publishing Co., Ltd.
PUBLISHER: Lin Gengli
PUBLISHING DIRECTOR: Lin Shijian
CHIEF EDITOR: Lin Shijian
DESIGN ADVISOR: Chen Ting
EXECUTIVE EDITOR: Alice Wu
EXECUTIVE ART EDITOR: Chun Sumkei
PROOFREADING: Judith Cressy, Li Weiji

REGISTERED ADDRESS: Room 15A Block 9 Tsui Chuk Garden, Wong Tai Sin, Kowloon, Hong Kong
TEL: +852-35832323 / **FAX:** +852-35832448
OFFICE ADDRESS: 7F, NO.9-1 Anning Street, Jinshazhou, Baiyun District, Guangzhou, China
TEL: +86-20-89095121 / **FAX:** +86-20-89095206
BEIJING OFFICE: Flat 1701, Block C, BBMG International, Wangjing West Road no.48, Chaoyang District, Beijing, China
TEL: +86-10-84139071 / **FAX:** +86-10-84139071
SHANGHAI OFFICE: Room 302, Floor 3, Ningbo Road no.349, Huangpu District, Shanghai, China
TEL: +86-21-63523469 / **FAX:** +86-21-63523469

SALES TEAM:
UK, Europe, Africa, Oceania: Sunnie sales02@sendpoints.cn
America, the Middle East: Mia sales03@sendpoints.cn
Asia: Hedy sales01@sendpoints.cn
TEL: +86-20-81007895
EMAIL: sales@sendpoints.cn
WEBSITE: www.sendpoints.cn / www.spbooks.cn

ISBN 978-988-79283-4-8

Printed and bound in China.

CONTENTS

ORIGIN AND HISTORY

Découpage

Origami

Parchment Craft

Paper Models

Paper Sculpture

Paper Cutting

Collage

Pop-up Books

Papier Mâché

Quilling

Collage

Collage is an art form produced by cutting, assembling, juxtaposing, and gluing pieces of paper, cloth, photographs, and other items onto a dry, flat surface. One of the most common materials used in collage is paper, including bits of newspaper, cutouts from magazine illustrations, sheet music, advertising brochures, and packaging.

Although Chinese artists applied the collage-like technique of juxtaposing and pasting separate pieces of paper to create borders for paintings during the Three Kingdoms (222-280 CE), and later occasionally used the technique for other purposes, it's the beginning of the 20th century that witnessed its transformation into an art form, of which Georges Braque (1882-1963) and Pablo Picasso (1881-1973), two pioneers of Cubism, were the most important contributors. Coined by Braque and Picasso, the term "collage" is derived from a French word, meaning "to glue", which clearly points out the core of the technique.

Beginning around 1912, Braque and Picasso were experimenting with combining common materials, such as paper and wood chips, with painting. *Still life with Chair Caning*, created by Picasso in 1912, is widely acknowledged as a classic of modern collage, in which a piece of oilcloth with caning pattern was pasted onto the canvas where still life objects are painted. Picasso and Braque practiced their concept of Cubism by incorporating collage materials into paintings, subverting the traditional perception that painting be two-dimensional in form, enriching canvas with multiple layers of items and meaning, and blurring the boundary between art and reality.

Dadaists further explored the content of collage, incorporating additional human elements into the mix, such as representations of human organs and portraits, etc. The famous Dada artist Kurt Schwitters (1887-1948) invented his own style of collage called Merz, which has become a signature of Dadaism. His works unified a wide range of materials, including transportation tickets, candy wrappers, calendars, leaflets, maps, and so on.

On the heels of Dadaists, Surrealist artists also constructed bizarre collage scenes with photographs, illustrations, and colored papers, creating a dreamy and fanciful realm.

Collage has undergone a series of changes under the influence of Cubism, Dada, Surrealism, and Constructivism, gradually becoming one of the most distinctive expressions of modern art. Not only does the mixture of different materials lend a rich texture, but the layered content can imbue collage works with deeper meanings.

Through collage, creators can free themselves from a traditional fixed perspective and create a collision between seemingly unconnected elements that originate from different standpoints. In this way, an artist can endow layers of meaning and bring endless possibilities to works of collage, which, for collage lovers, is perhaps the reason it is so fascinating.

[1]

Source: Wiki
Designer: Polly Glott

Paper Models

A paper model is constructed by cutting, folding, and gluing together pieces of paper, card stock, or cardboard to create a simulated—and usually small—version of a ship, plane, vehicle, building, animal, or other inspiring object.

[II]

The first paper models were probably designed as toys for children: The appearance of a paper model printed in a French toy catalogue in 1800 is considered one of the earliest commercial paper-model products. With the development of new printing presses and the production of inexpensive paper during the Industrial Revolution (1760-1840), printed paper products became accessible and convenient and were soon a mainstay in the manufacture of toys. Publishing companies started to produce colorful paper model kits with enough individual pieces to cut out, glue together, and create a complete scene.

In the middle of the 19th century, Imagerie d'Épinal Pellerin, a French publishing company, launched hundreds of realistic paper models of buildings, scenery, activities, figures, and vehicles, which helped children learn about places and events around the world. The German company Schreiber-Verlag also contributed importantly to the development of paper building models. Verlag-Schreiber's paper theaters notably set the standard for theater toys, and its models of buildings and historical events were used as educational tools in schools. Schreiber's models, also well-known for reflecting German historical events, were frequently used as educational tools in schools. The innovative toys designed by these publishing companies stimulated the popularity of paper models throughout Europe, attracting adult interest as well as that of children.

In the early 20th century, many European magazines included inserts of printed advertising cards designed to be cut out and assembled as models. An unprecedented enthusiasm for paper models arose during WWII, when paper was one of the few materials that wasn't rationed. However, this also led to the craft's decline in popularity when rationing was lifted at the end of the war. Micromodels that were no bigger than a postcard and could be stored in a shoe box were a particular fad during wartime.

Among all types of paper model, military scale model kits, created to the same scale as their counterparts during the First World War, were specifically designed for and loved by teenage boys interested in military technology, weapons, ships and aircraft. Gradually, the production of scale-model kits has become a full-blown industry covering a broad range of products, from vehicles and architecture, to animated figures.

Indeed, using a two-dimensional template to create a miniature three-dimensional replica of something that captures your interest is such a magical process that it rewards all the labor and thought that goes into piecing together hundreds of small components. Small wonder that, today, there are a number of companies producing paper templates for model builders: In fact, some enthusiasts even start from scratch and build their own templates. It is a craft that evolves with the technology of each new age, creating new avenues for exploration and developing, always, as an interesting means to express originality and artistry.

[II]
Source: Wiki
Designer: Stina Hedvall

[III]
Source: Wiki
Designer: Kim Traynor

[III]

Découpage

[IV]

The term découpage comes from Middle French, meaning "to cut out". Decoupage refers to the art of embellishing an object by gluing pictures cut from paper onto the surface, which subsequently will be coated with paint, varnish, gold leaf, and other materials.

[V]

In ancient times, nomadic tribes in easten Siberia cut out felt to decorate tombs. It is one of the earliest known uses of the découpage technique. In the 12th century, the craft made its way to China where it was applied to more ordinary items such as lanterns, windows, boxes and so on.

In the 17th century, artisans in Venice were among the first to become acquainted with this craft, through their frequent trade with the Far East. Lacquerware and lacquered furniture were highly fashionable in Venice at that time. To meet an enormous demand that outweighed the supply, artisans began to create counterfeit lacquer works as an alternative and cheaper offer. They cut out sheets of hand-colored engravings and prints, adhered them to the surface of furniture, and applied layers of varnish to create a high-gloss finish similar to those of genuine lacquer works. At first, works by master artists were chosen for the paper cutouts, but before long, works by less famous artists were also employed due to the growing demand and economical considerations, which is why decoupage was called *l'arte del povero* – poor man's arts.

In fact, a number of other craft skills grew in importance as they developed along with the popularity of découpage. In 1760, a book entitled *The Ladies Amusement* or *The Whole Art of Japanning Made Easy* was published to teach gentlewomen how to color, to glue, and to varnish the pictures they had découpaged. Mary Delany (1700-1788), a confidante of King George III and Queen Charlotte of England, was a talented artist who produced exquisite decoupage works with cutouts of delicate reproductions of plants and flowers. Her works, which brought decoupage to a higher level, are still preserved in the British Museum.

By the 1960s, decoupage had made its way across the Atlantic, and Americans were starting to decoupage ordinary household items into beautiful works of art. Today, decoupage is experiencing a renaissance throughout the world, and this centuries-old technique with its infinite possibilities is still inspiring incredible works of art.

[IV]

Source: Wiki
Designer: Mary Delany

[V]

Source: Wiki
Designer: Durova

Parchment Craft

Parchment craft, also called pergamano ("perga" for parchment and "mano" for hands in Spanish), refers to the art of creating delicate, lace-like designs in parchment or vellum papers through the use of various techniques, including embossing, perforating, outlining, stippling, cutting, coloring, and blending.

[VI]

True parchment is made from animal skins that have been stretched and scraped to translucency. Because the material is durable, it has been used in some areas of Africa for making masks, clothing, and drums. In medieval Europe it was used as a writing surface, particularly for hymnbooks and other religious books of folio size.

The making of thin, strong parchment had reached a remarkable level of craftsmanship by the 4th century. Early decorative parchment craft appeared at least by the 15th century, applied to the decorative edges of pages and bindings of books in Spanish cloisters.

By the 16th century, paper had replaced parchment, even in religious books, but the decorative craft of embellishment continued. Paper parchment craft was widely used in European countries, such as Germany, Belgium, and Holland, appearing as lace-like decoration.

With the relocation of missionaries and settlers, the craft was introduced into Catholic communities in South America and its vitality grew in the South American culture. It was due to the influence of French Romanticism in the 19th century that more romantic elements and themes were added to the parchment craft. For instance, the subjects of cherubs and flowers appeared along with relief and three-dimensional effects.

The popularity of modern parchment craft in the 20th century was bound up with Martha Ospina, a Columbian girl who started to learn the craft when she was 14. When she married a Dutchman, she resettled in Holland, where she began to teach the craft to local people. Martha made great contributions to the development of parchment skills and the refinement of precision tools. She also published books of patterns, thus encouraging the reappearance of the craft in Europe, and its application to all sorts of paper goods.

The parchment paper we use today is treated to appear translucent, like the original thin animal-skin parchment, and parchment craft is burgeoning in popularity. Enjoyed in Europe, Japan, Australia, South Africa, and Canada, and growing in popularity in the U.S, the craft is widely applied to making bookmarks, photo frames, lampshades, gift boxes, and other decorative objects.

[VI]
Source: Wiki

Pop-up Books

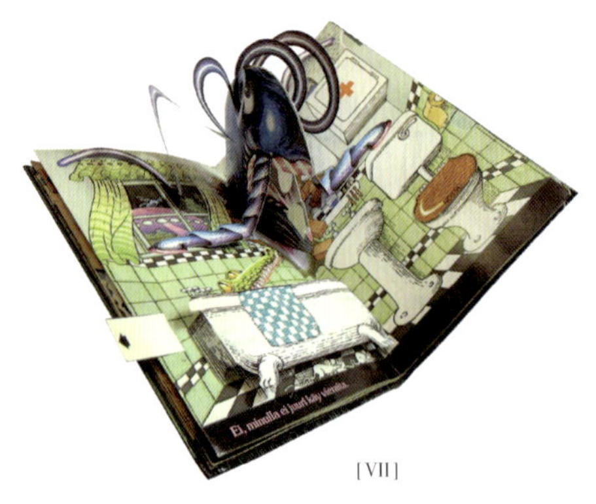

[VII]

The pop-up book is a paper-engineered creation that combines the functions of a picture book and a paper toy. Pop-ups include the text and illustrations of an ordinary book but the spreads share a space with clever, precision-engineered mechanisms that enhance the story. These are a popular source of fancy and delight that provide an unconventional interactive experience and playful, three dimensional displays.

The first known book with movable parts dates back to the mid-13th century when Matthew Paris, an English Benetictine monk, added a mechanical device to the pages of the *Chronica Majora*. In compiling this book, Matthew had to include so many calculations for the dates of important Christian holidays, that the effort he put into searching for dates was occupying a huge amount of his time. To make the references more convenient, he transferred the data onto a revolving parchment disc, or volvelle, which marked the beginning of paper-engineering history.

In 1775, Thomas Malton published *A Compleat Treatise on Perspective in Theory and Practice*, which is the earliest documented, commercially produced pop-up book. At that time movables were primarily marketed to adults, mainly as teaching tools in scholarly works. That changed in the late 18th century, when publisher Robert Sayer produced a selection of paper-engineered books called "harlequinades" or "turn-up" books, to delight children. The format of his books, now known as "metamorphoses books" included lift-the-flap attachments to each illustration so that the reader could change the image and advance the story while creating amusing variations in the scenes.

Books with three-dimensional activities and tab-activated pages were not published in great numbers until the 19th century, beginning in England and Germany. Tab-activated books allowed children to manipulate movement on a page with a slight pull on a paper tab.

Lothar Meggendorfer (1847-1925), a German illustrator, expanded on tab-activated movement and showed off his extraordinary talent for paper engineering by adding multiple actions to a page and refining the use of rivets and levers that brought the pages to life. Meggendorfer's stunning imagination and creativity won him a place among the geniuses of paper engineering for all time.

In the 20th century, English publisher S. Louis Giraud invented the Bookano Series, which featured a three-dimensional structure that could be viewed 360 degrees. The smaller scenes leap off the page when the book is opened. In the 1930s, Blue Ribbon Press, a Chicago-based publisher, copyrighted the term 'pop-up'.

Nowadays pop-up books have developed to a new level, through the contributions of many paper engineers and book designers. The combination of sophisticated illustrations and intricate mechanical devices has made pop-up books increasingly complex and popular.

[VIII]

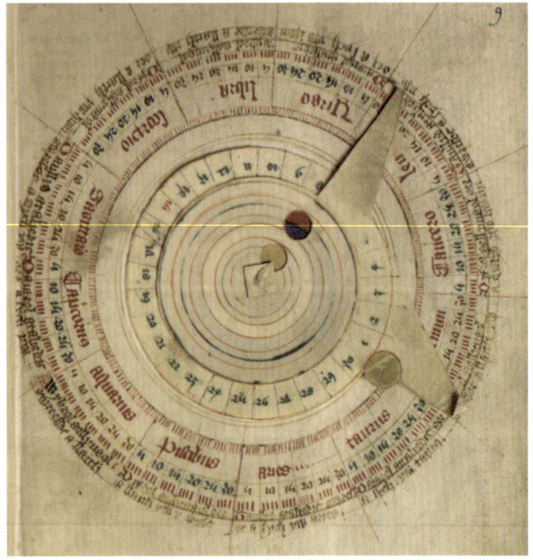

[VII]

Source: Wiki
Designer: Kim Viljanen

[VIII]

Source: Wiki
Designer: Gutun Owain

Origami

The Japanese word "origami", composed of "ori" from the verb "oru" (to fold) and "gami" from the noun "kami" (paper), means paper folding, and origami is the name use for this art form not just in Japan, but everywhere throughout the world. Earlier examples of paper folding could have many origins, but certainly one can be linked to the birthplace of papermaking—China. The Chinese "yuanbao" —paper folded to resemble gold nuggets, used at traditional funerals—is one of the earliest known uses for paper folding.

[IX]

After papermaking was introduced into Japan in the early 7th century, origami gradually gained popularity and grew to be a representative of Japanese culture. In the beginning, due to the complex and costly process of producing paper, origami was restrained to religious and ceremonial use. Folded paper butterflies were often used in ceremonies during the Heian period (794-1192). By the time of the Edo period (1603-1868), improvements in the papermaking process made paper more affordable to ordinary people and subsequently origami became a popular pastime.

Among the most classic origami forms are cranes, samurai helmets, and kusudama. In Japanese culture, a crane is an auspicious symbol of longevity. A string of 1,000 cranes called *senbazuru* is considered to have the power to free people from disease or natural disasters. Today *senbazuru* is still a popular means of showing encouragement and concern to those who are ill. A samurai helmet, which symbolizes strength and health is another typical origami form: On Boy's Day in Japan, a festival held on May 5, every family folds paper into Samurai helmet shapes to make wishes for their children's health and happiness. Some use newspaper to fold a samurai helmet large enough to wear on the head. As paper folding evolves, new branches spring up.

For instance, modular origami is created by assembling small pieces, mostly identical ones. Kusudama, is a classic form of Japanese modular origami, often seen as paper flowers that have been assembled from many parts and arranged in a ball shape. The idea comes from the folk custom of stringing up fresh flowers or herbs and putting them in small pouches to preserve their natural fragrance.

European methods of paper folding appear to be independent of Japanese origins, and developed much later. Paper folding in Europe has its own unique look and often features 45 degree folds, giving it more of a geometric or mathematical look than Japanese examples. Friedrich Fröbel (1782-1852), German inventor of kindergartens, explored paper folding from an educational perspective, and turned it into a creative means for teaching children. German paper folding came to Japan along with the kindergarten system during the Meiji period (1868-1912). The ideas of German paper folding influenced that of Japanese origami. Hence, modern Japanese origami is a combination of its own traditions and features of European paper folding.

Paper folding encountered some new changes in the 20th century. Lillian Oppenheimer (1898-1992), one of the founders of OrigamiUSA, popularized the word "origami" in western countries. In addition, a Japanese paper artist Akira Yoshizawa is credited with the new technique of wet-folding, as well as the international Yoshizawa–Randlett system notation for origami folds. With all these changes, origami is becoming professionalized and systematical. Today, the growing enthusiasm and interest for origami bring new ideas and techniques to the craft, and surely there is more to come.

[IX]

Source: Wiki
Designer: Jacek Halicki

Paper Sculpture

Paper sculpture is a three-dimensional form of artwork that is made from multiple layers of paper, and then shaped by hand or with tools. There are no particular rules for sculpting paper, nor limits to the selection of materials. Because of paper's fragility, designers often include elements of stone, metal, wood, or ceramics to fortify the structure of paper sculptures and to help maintain them. In fact any variety of substances and tools can be used in the process of creating paper sculptures, a freedom that encourages imagination and endless artistic possibilities.

The art of paper sculpture grew out of the practice of origami, which developed in Japan after Chinese Buddhist monks introduced the craft of papermaking there around the 6th century. Origami has been deeply rooted in Japan's traditional culture ever since, with many master craftsmen contributing new techniques and forms to the practice. One of these was paper sculpture, which was soon copied in the West.

During the 17th and 18th centuries, enthusiastic artists around Europe designed ingenious paper sculptures, drawing from many themes. The artists' careful selections of paper tones and their awareness of the effects of light and shadow in the works suggests their regard for the medium. Among these artists was British sculptor Augustine Walker, whose works are still displayed in the Maritime Museum in Greenwich, England.

Today the art of creating paper sculpture can be enjoyed by professionals, amateurs, and folk artists through the expansion of modern media. The many instructional videos and books enable paper sculpture lovers to explore all the possibilities of the craft. In schools and universities around the world, classes in paper sculpture not only help students acquire the necessary technical skills, but they help pass on the craft to a new generation.

Paper sculpture is now commonly appreciated as a form of domestic decoration and it plays a role in commercial illustration, as well as in industrial and graphic design.

[X]

Designer: Mathilde Nive

Paper Cutting

Paper cutting, as a kind of paper art, can trace its origin back to the Eastern Han Dynasty in China (25-220). Around AD 105, papermaking was invented by a royal Chinese court official called Cai Lun, and the birth of paper cutting followed. According to relics that have been unearthed, the earliest existing example of paper cutting is a symmetrical circle from the Six Dynasties (222-589) found in Xinjiang, China.

[XI]

[XI]

Source: Wiki
Designer: AgataSz

As a traditional folk art in China, paper cutting has a particular cultural appeal. Variations drawn from many elements over a long history have redefined and enriched the cultural expression of Chinese paper cutting, including Chinese characters, human figures, scenes from folk tales and so forth. The conception of paper cutting mirrors how the Chinese express their wishes for a better life through homophonic and symbolic allusions. For instance, a design featuring a fish symbolizes a prosperous year as the Chinese word "鱼"(fish) is a phonetic equivalent of "余"(more than enough); a paper-cut design showing a crane under a pine tree indicates longevity as both objects symbolize a long and happy life. With its meticulous craftsmanship and auspicious implications, paper cutting presents itself frequently in festive occasions like the Chinese New Year, weddings, and child birth. For over a thousand years, paper cutting has spread and developed as a carrier of Chinese folk custom and wisdom. Nowadays, it has become an indispensable part of Chinese culture.

Paper cutting met diverse cultures as papermaking spread. In Japan, paper cutting is called *kirie* or *kirigami*. Around AD 800, the flourishing papermaking industry enabled paper cutting to flourish. During the Edo period (1603-1868), *kamikiri*, a performing art derived from paper cutting, came onto the stage. Performers usually cut out shapes requested by a live audience on the spot, sometimes accompanied by music or limited by time. Since the artisans are not allowed to draft the patterns in advance, *Kamikiri* is considered to be a demanding form of paper cutting.

It was not until the 12th century that papermaking was developed in Europe. The relatively late introduction of papermaking did not render Europe backward in artistic expression or skills in terms of paper cutting. Since the Middle Ages, Jewish paper cutting has been a folk art with its own symbolism, employing a variety of animals like lions, snakes, deer, and birds. In addition, it has played a role in Jewish traditional customs and ceremonies. For example, Jewish paper cutting can serve as decoration of Ketubot (Jewish marriage contracts). German paper cutting, also called Scherenschnitte, is characterized by symmetrical patterns. By folding the paper intricately before cutting, it represents dimensional and complex ways of paper cutting. It is often used for decoration on legal documents and at festivals such as Christmas and Easter.

In modern times, paper cutting remains extremely popular as an art form. The craft has been enriched by an increasing number of styles and patterns, and more potential is derived from the combination of paper cutting with art techniques like stenciling. Having lasted more than a thousand years, paper cutting is a timeless craft of tangible beauty.

Papier Mâché

[XII]

Papier mâché, known as "chewed paper" or "pulped paper" involves the reuse of mashed up paper or strips to mold a new form. There are two ways to create a craft from papier mâché. When the paper is soaked through, use the mashed pulp to cover the surface of the support you are working on. As soon as it has dried thoroughly, it's ready for your next steps.The second method is to pour the mix of paper pulp and glue into or over a prepared mold to create the desired shape. Let it dry and then apply the next steps of painting, varnishing, or lacquering.

One of papier mâché's great advantages is that its mix of paper pulp and glue produces a lightweight but strong material. The technique has been applied to creating a wide range of products including bowls, trays, boxes, and furniture.

Research has turned up relics such as helmets and pot lids that were created of papier mâché in China as early as the Han Dynasty (206 BC-220). The paper technique spread to Japan and Persia, and much later, to Europe, where it enjoyed a golden age.

In the 17th century, the French recognized the potential for papier mâché, using it to make snuff bottles and other decorative objects, imitating the look and texture of plaster or stone. The English followed suit and explored new ways to use papier mâché such as making it into a waterproof material, using it as a structural material in building, and using it for furniture.

In Birmingham, England, papier mâché trays, tables, and wall decorations were mass produced in factories. Because of its low costs, there was a huge demand for papier mâché in construction applications throughout Europe in the 18th and 19th centuries.

Today one of the material's common uses is in large-scale sculptures, for such purposes as carnival floats and theater sets, which have to be constructed quickly and inexpensively.

[XIII]

[XII]

Source: Wiki
Designer: Unknown

[XIII]

Designer: Cesar Leal

Quilling

Quilling or paper filigree is an art form where strips of paper that are rolled, looped, curled and twisted are combined in a variety of ways to make an intricate design. Within the range of paper arts, quilling presents a unique style, distinguished by its refined look and complexity. The beauty of the art is in its elaborate details: the texture of the coils, the dynamic lines after curling, the visual effect of arranging coils in a specific order, as well as the color matching of paper strips. People can enjoy quilling for many aesthetic reasons.

The origin of the term "quilling" is still being debated. Some believe that it got its name because the shapes were made with the aid of a quill way back in Europe's past. In any case, the art has been around for centuries, with its development largely in Europe. During the Renaissance, French and Italian nuns and monks trimmed strips from gilded edges of books to create filigree decorations for religious articles as an alternative to costly gold and silver crafts.

By the 18th century, quilling reached its golden peak. It was considered a kind of fashionable pastime in England and enjoyed great popularity among upper-class and middle-class ladies. Much of the quilling they produced was used to embellish tea boxes and coasters. Meanwhile, this paper art spread to the American colonies where it was used as a means to decorate pictures, trays, boxes, and other items. Often, the technique was combined with other art forms including embroidery and painting, and was paired with sparkling materials such as shell, pearls, and mica flakes.

Today quilling is still practiced and has developed through the popularity of tutorials and craft classes. It is a simple craft to master and an affordable hobby that can be enjoyed by people of all ages and walks of life. As practitioners advance through the techniques, quilling art can be mesmerizing: and the craft can be used to create stand-alone pieces as well as for decorating other art work. Quilling has developed into a mature art form and more and more people will be attracted to its charms.

[XIV]

Source: Wiki
Designer: Inna Dorman

PAPERCRAFT TECHNIQUES

Commonly Used Tools

❶ An X-acto knife has a variety of replaceable blades, among which the #11 Blade is frequently used for cutting paper details. ❷ Scissors are used for cutting paper into the desired size. ❸ A scalpel is sharper than a box cutter and is used for detailed and delicate cutting; but the tool is expensive, and the blades become dull quickly. ❹ A box cutter is used for cutting paper into the desired size and shape. ❺ A sharp circular blade is suitable for cutting paper, cloth, etc. ❻ A cutting plotter has many functions, such as lettering, hollowing out, hollowing, and drawing, which can reduce, the manual labor. ❼ A laser cutter outfitted with smooth cut, high precision, fast speed, can produce continuous and repetitive cutting work.

8 White glue is suitable for paper, wood, cloth, and leather pasting. It has strong adhesion, high speed of drying, and good waterproof performance. 9 A glue stick is easy to apply, and keeps the surface neat and clean, yet it has relatively weak adhesion. 10 Hot glue is eco-friendly, safe, waterproof and dries quickly. 11 Liquid glue allows for quick attachment of paper to surfaces but can cause wrinkling and ripping. 12 Transparent adhesive tape won't affect the beauty of artworks, and it adheres well. 13 A cutting mat can protect the blade and prevent the desktop from becoming scratched during cutting. The grid line on the mat can provide reference for drawing and cutting direction. 14 A ruler can assist in drawing and measuring length.

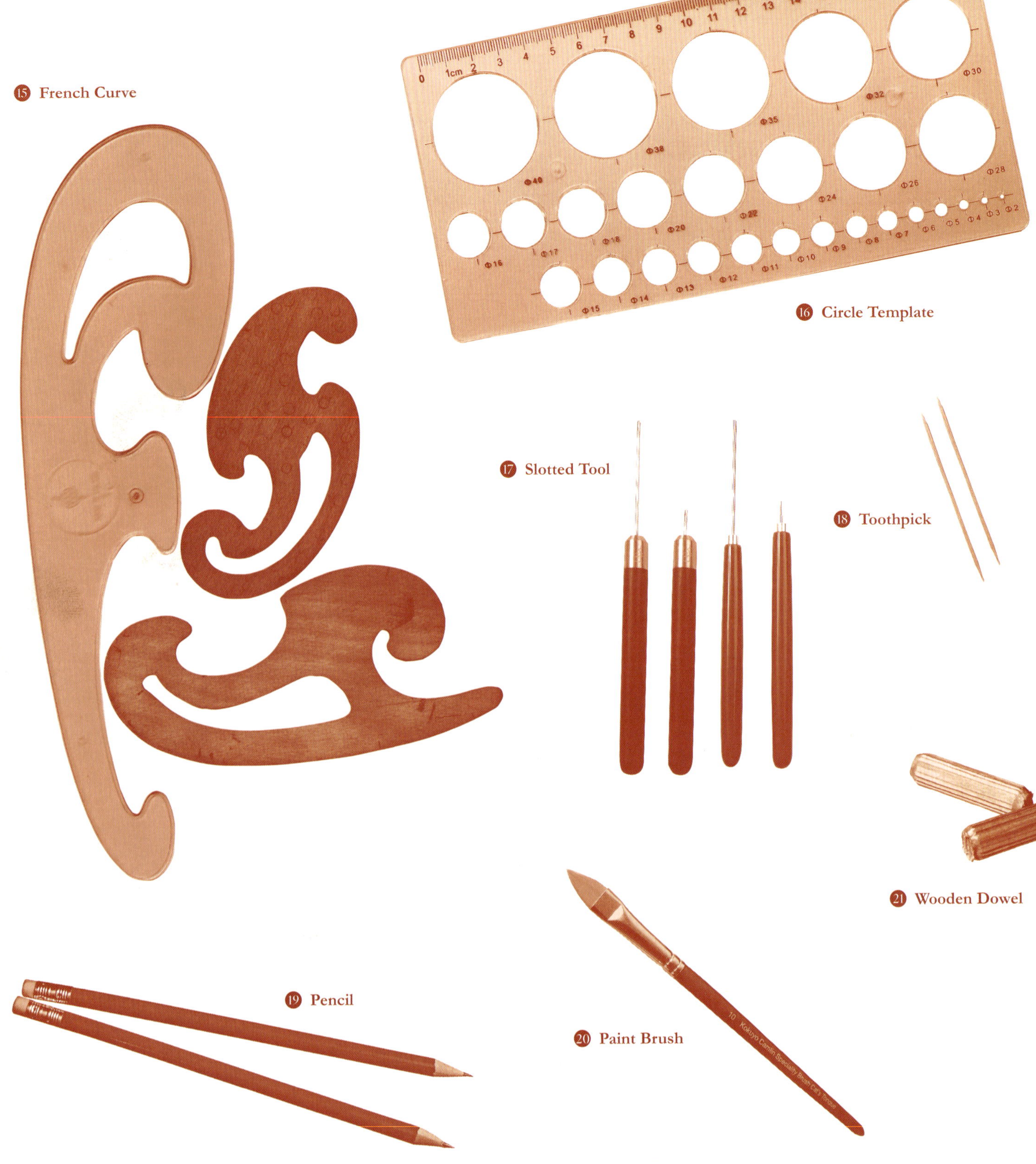

⑮ A French curve is used for drawing smooth curves. Draw the number of points, and then use the curve board to connect them into a line. ⑯ A circle template, used in quilling, has holes of different sizes that are useful for adjusting and unifying the sizes of paper coils. ⑰ A slotted tool is an important tool for paper quilling. Insert the end of strip in its slot, roll the tool and create the quilling coils. ⑱ A toothpick is used mainly for spreading glue and adjusting small parts. ⑲ A pencil is used for designing and drawing thumbnail sketches, and for making shadow and pasting locations. ⑳ A paint brush is useful for paint, water, glue, and more. ㉑ A wooden dowel is used for connecting the parts and fastening the joints. ㉒ An engraving burin is used for paper-cutting with two kinds of blades, an oblique point and a round edge. ㉓ A roller can apply paints to a large area. ㉔ Tweezers are useful for fixing, shaping and assembling models. Choose tweezers with pointed tips for manipulating bits of paper.

25 Cardstock is a relatively heavy paper that is flexible, springy, and slightly stiff, allowing you to shape it into various paper forms; Foamcore can serve as a carving or filling material; Corflute is actually plastic that is as thin as paper, with a lattice structure that is lightweight, transparent, and hard to scratch; Carbon paper is placed between sheets of paper to transfer designs or wriitng from one to the other; Washi paper is light but durable, with fine and beautiful texture, suitable for all kinds of paper design; Golden foil has metallic luster and strong adhesion, and is used as decoration of paper crafts; Tracing paper can be used as sketch paper, but its translucency allows you to see through it to other layers of a design.

Cutting

Cutting, an important technique in in creating paper artworks, requires patience and meticulous care. Take time to cut out patterns carefully along their outlines to guarantee smooth, finished edges. In addition to cutting a single sheet of paper, you can fold a sheet before cutting it, thus resulting in identical designs on both sides of the fold. Different types of folds will result in different effects.

Symmetric Folding and Cutting (1 Axis of Symmetry)

1. Fold a square piece of paper in half, side-to-side, or along the diagonal. Crease the fold.

2. Draw the desired shape or design on the top layer, remembering that the fold will be the center of the design.

3. Cut out the shape with scissors. Keep your cutting hand steady as you turn the paper with your other hand.

4. Open the fold for the final shape.

3-sided Fold and Cut (3 Axes of Symmetry)

1. Begin with a square sheet of paper and fold it in half diagonally. Then fold it again.

2. Unfold the paper. Fold the bottom right corner to the center crease and unfold.

3. Bring the left-hand edge down along the crease mark from step 2. Unfold it to get the second crease. Fold the second crease to the first crease to get the third crease in between.

4. Take the left corner and make an angled fold upwards to the point of the third crease on the right edge.Turn the figure over, and take the other corner and fold it along the bottom edge.

4-sided Fold and Cut (4 Axes of Symmetry)

1. Take a square paper and fold it in half twice.

2. Fold it diagonally or fold the paper along the diagonal three successive times. This is a recommended way to avoid mistakes.

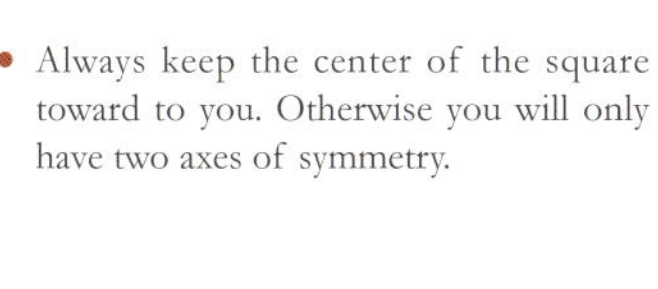

- Always keep the center of the square toward to you. Otherwise you will only have two axes of symmetry.

5-sided Fold and Cut (5 Axes of Symmetry)

1. Fold a square of paper in half twice, side to side to create a center fold. Open the second fold and place the paper in front of you with the first fold along the top edge. Bring the bottom left.

2. Fold it in half again to make another crease and unfold it. Mark the point with a pencil.

3. Take the right-hand corner and fold it over to the point. Fold the corner back on itself so it meets the right edge.

4. Make another corner fold along the edge of the right side. Fold it over so that the edges meet.

5. Fold down the corner and unfold. Cut off the excess paper. Open the paper to gain a five-pointed star.

6-sided Fold and Cut (6 Axes of Symmetry)

Create a 3-sided fold and then fold it in half.

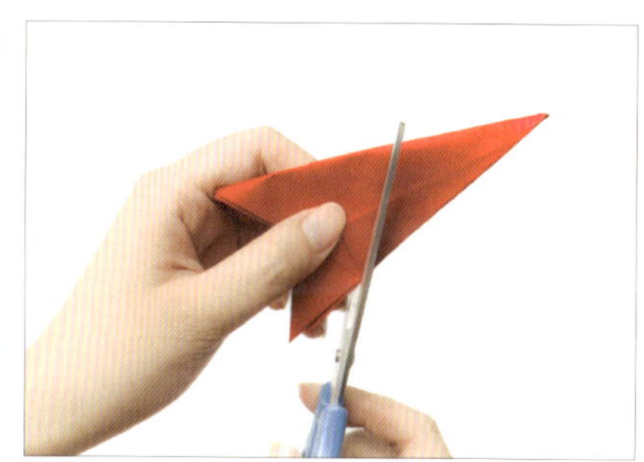

8-sided Fold and Cut (8 Axes of Symmetry)

Create a 4-sided fold. Then fold in the left-hand point toward the right-hand fold.

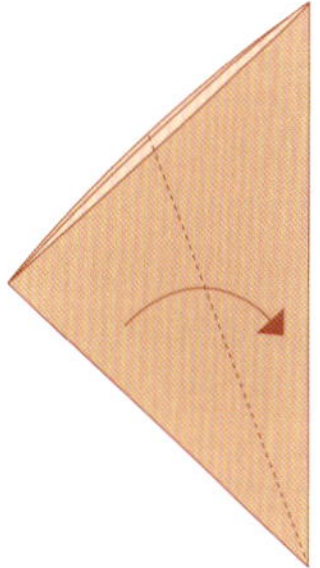

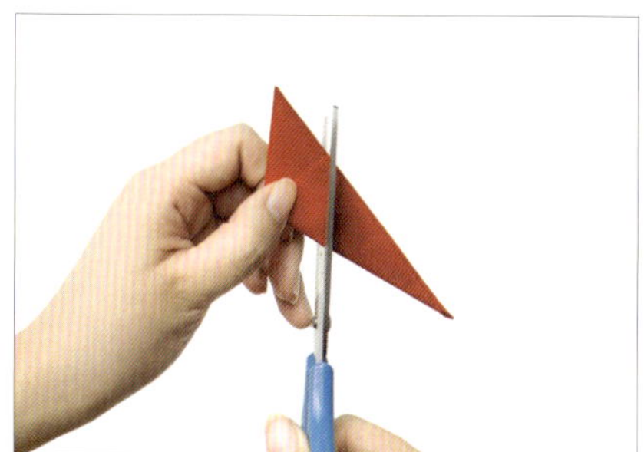

Folding

Folding is one of the most fundamental papercraft techniques, allowing you to shape and construct objects without destroying the integrity of the paper. Traditional folding techniques are done without tools, but that has changed and the limits on tools and techniques have broken down as more elements are engaged in modern origami. All kinds of everyday paper—newspaper, construction paper, wrapping paper, and more—can be used for folding. As soon as you have a piece of paper in your hand, you can begin to enjoy the pleasure of origami.

- A bone folder is not necessary but is definitely a convenient auxiliary tool. Use the tip of the tool to trace your folding lines before making the folds, and use the side of the tool to flatten folds and sharpen the creases.

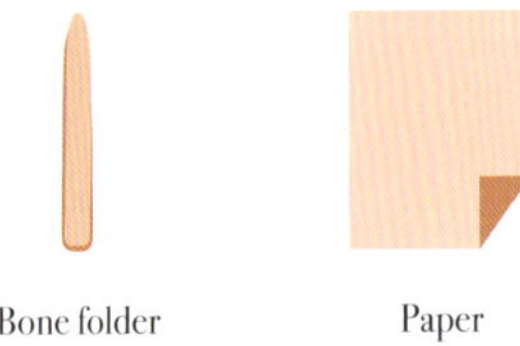

Bone folder   Paper

Origami Symbols

The Yoshizawa–Randlett system is an international system of folding symbols. Most tutorials employ these symbols to help instructions. Familiarizing yourself with the symbols and their meanings will help you learn the folding process.

Lines: All sorts of creases

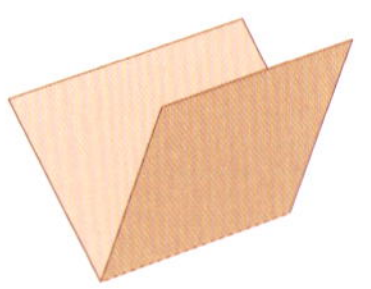

Dashed line: it indicates where the paper will be folded upward. Dashed lines often indicate valley folds.

Dash-dot-dot line or dash-dot line: it indicates the fold is made by making the fold downward, to the back. It is often called the mountain fold.

Black line: it indicates a fold that has been creased and then unfolded.

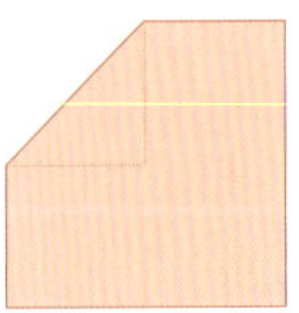

Dotted line: it indicates the position of a fold on the back side of paper.

Arrow: Directionality of folding

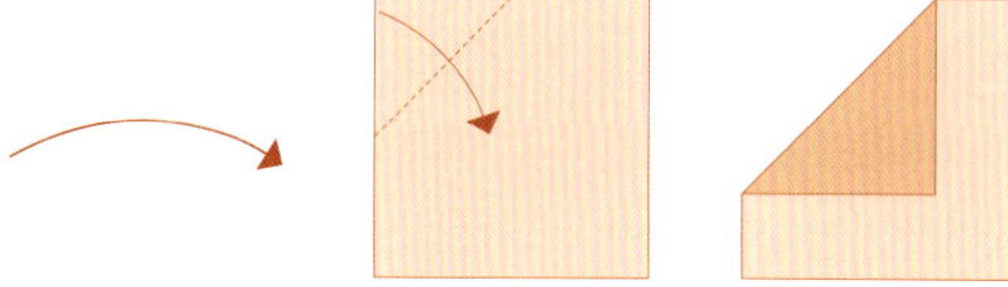

Full arrow: this indicates a fold to the front of the sheet of paper. It usually appears with a dashed line (valley fold).

Hollow arrow: this shows a fold to the back side of the sheet of paper. It often appears with a dash-dot-dot line (mountain fold).

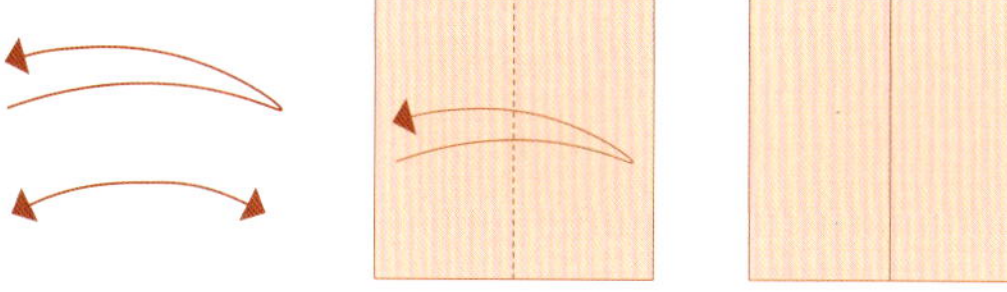

Double arrow: this tells you to fold and unfold to form a crease.

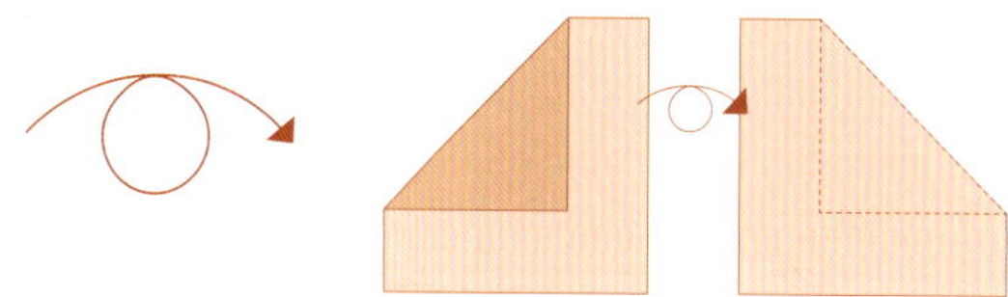

Loop-the-loop arrow: this tells you to turn the figure over.

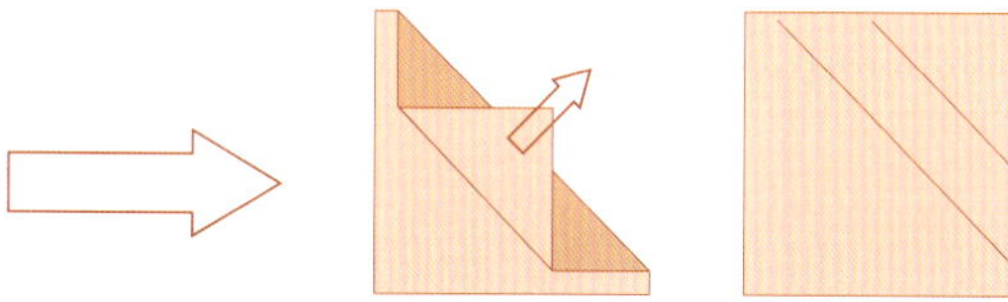

Large and hollow arrow: this tells you to open out a fold.

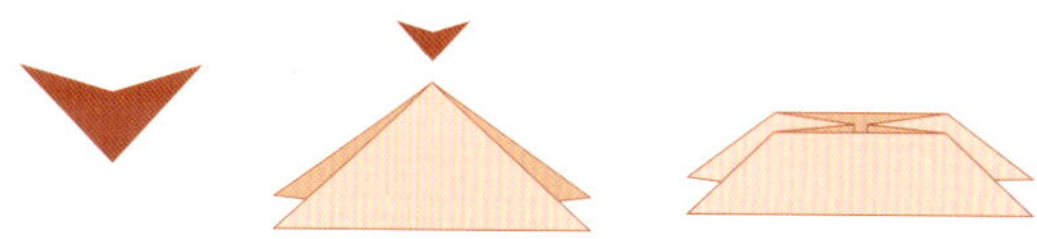

Solid arrow head: this tells you to insert and flatten a fold.

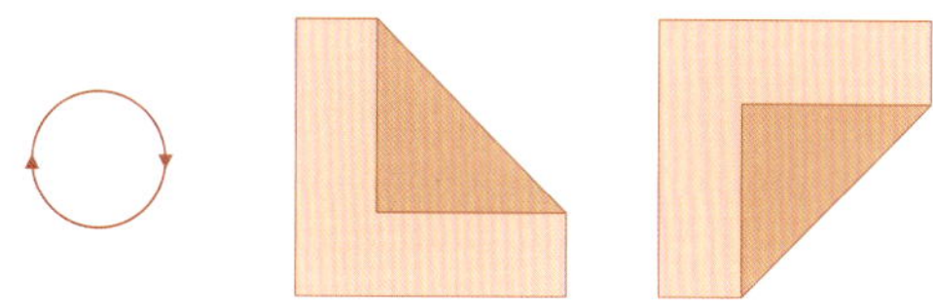

Rotating arrow: this indicates to rotate the sheet of paper to a certain degree.

Inflated arrow : this tells you to inflate the model, making it 3-D.

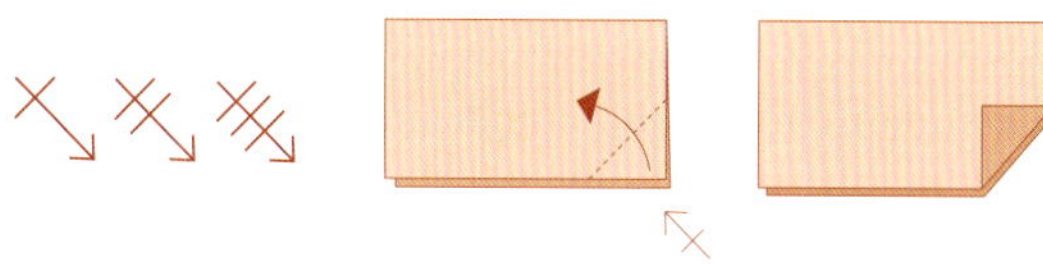

Arrow with crossed lines: this tells you to repeat a fold at the indicated spot. The number of crossed lines on the arrow tells you how many times to repeat the action.

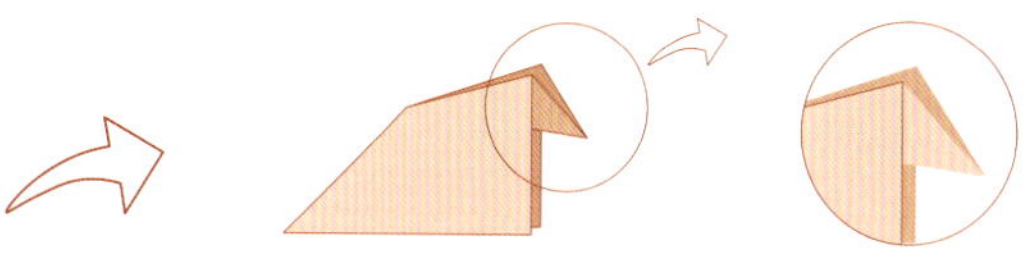

Zoom-in arrow: this indicates a close-up illustration of a small section or fold.

Origami Bases

Many origami creations begin with the most basic, recurring folds. These are the origami bases. Mastering the bases will make learning origami and becoming comfortable with advanced folding much easier.

Square Base

- This is also called the preliminary fold. It is the bread and butter of origami.

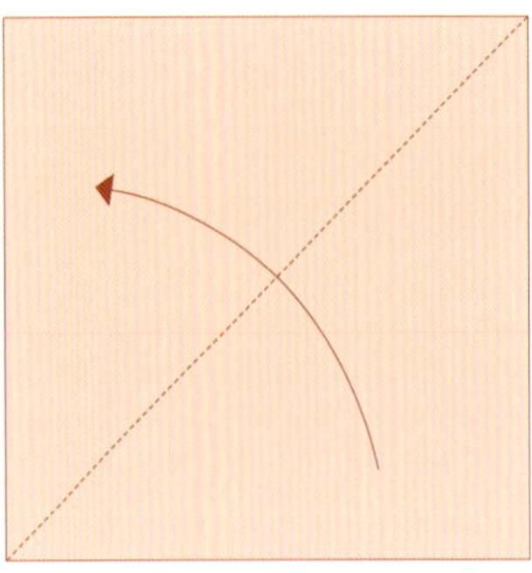

1. Fold the square paper in half diagonally to make a triangle.

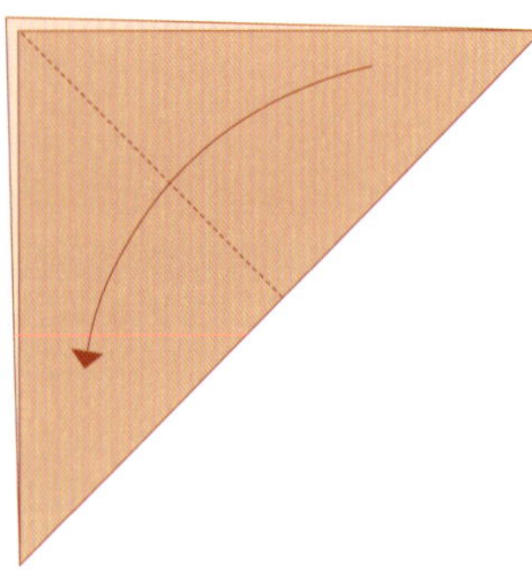

2. Fold the triangle again.

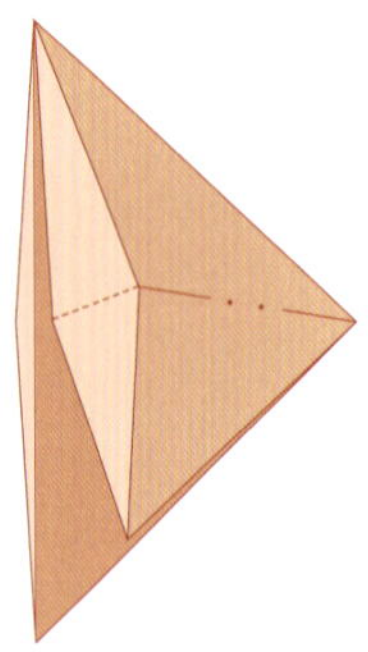

3. Open out the top triangular section into a square.

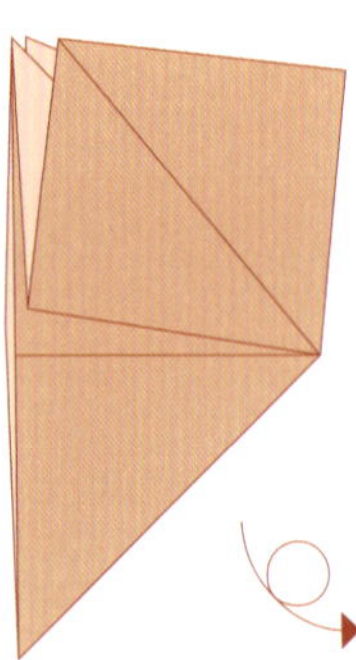

4. Turn the model over.

5. Repeat step 3.

Kite Base

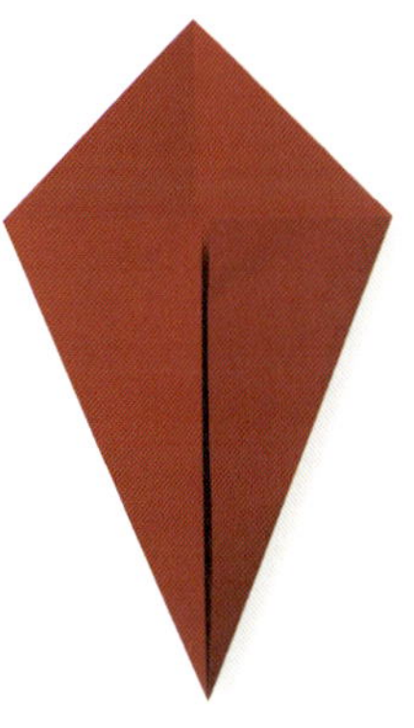

- This origami base looks just like a kite.

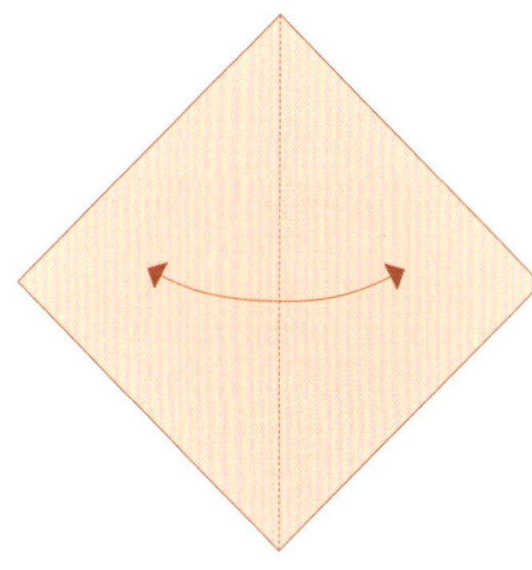

1. Fold the square paper in haft diagonally to get a crease. Unfold.

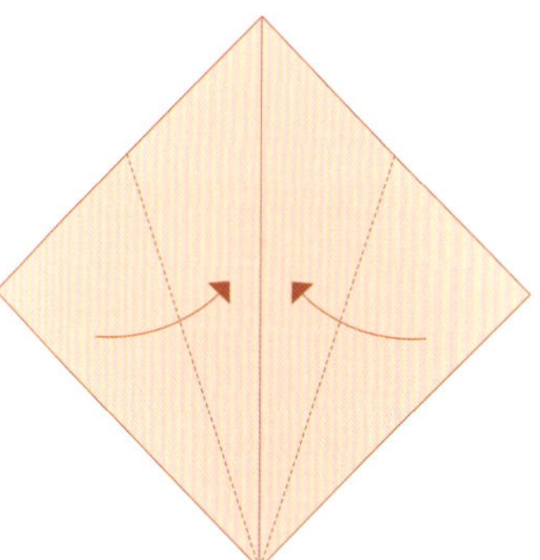

2. Fold the lower edges of right and left corners to align with the central crease.

Balloon Base

- The triangle base is also known as the balloon or waterbomb base.

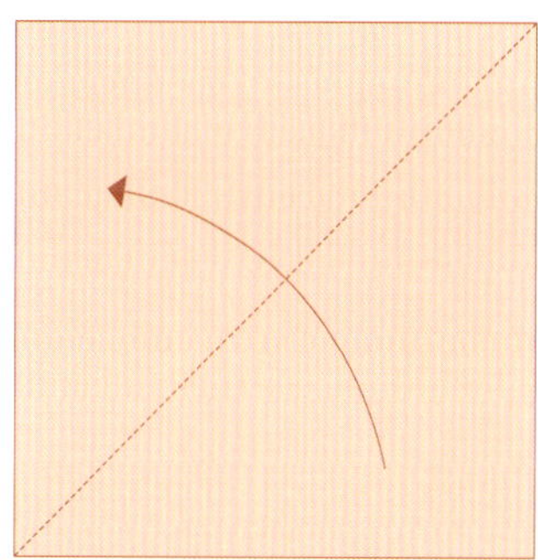

1. Fold the square of paper in half diagonally to make a triangle.

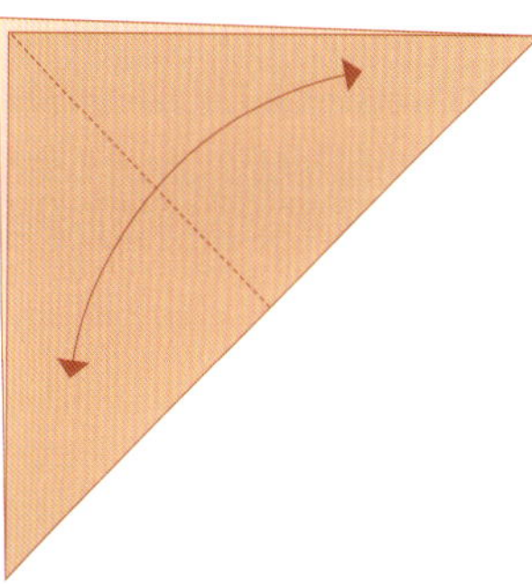

2. Fold the triangle. Open all the folds so that the paper is square.

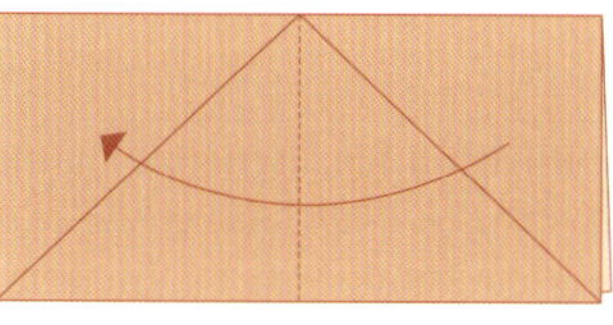

3. Fold the paper in half top to bottom. Fold it in half, left to right.

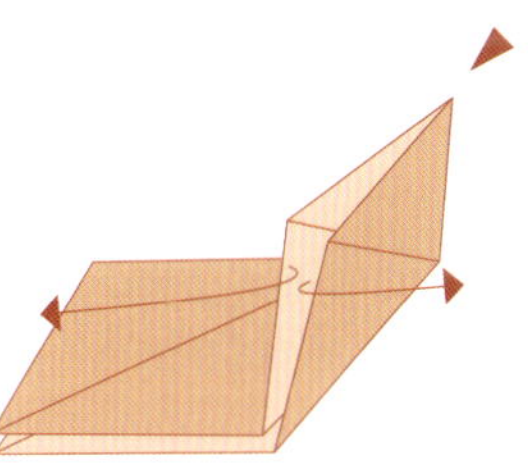

4. Open out the top square section along the diagonal fold lines.

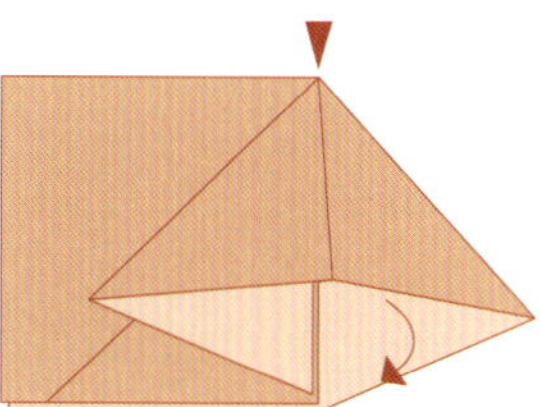

5. Flatten it to form a triangle.

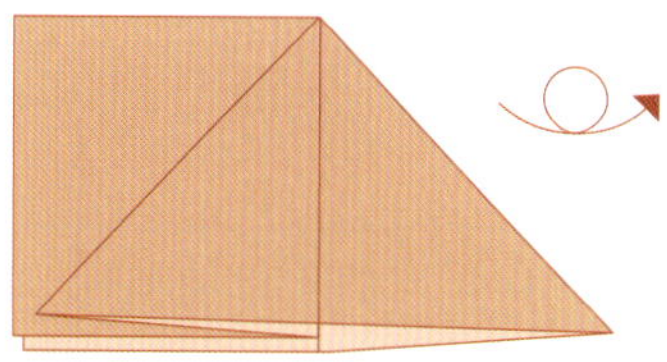

6. Turn the model over and repeat steps 4 and 5.

Bird Base

- This is the foundation for folding many origami birds, including the crane.

1. Make a square base, rotate the open side of the figure toward you.

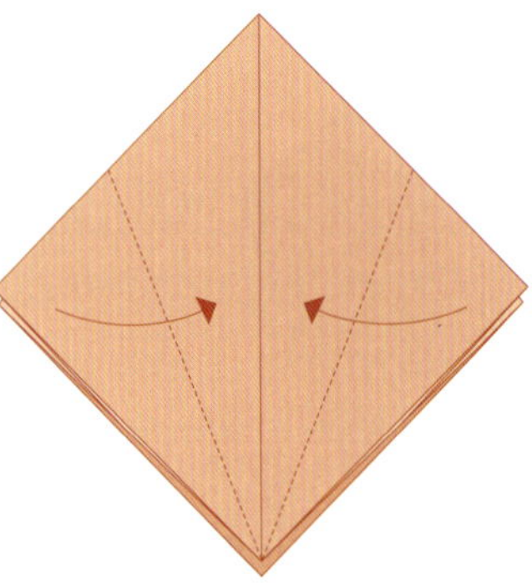

2. Fold the right and left corners of the top square to align with the central crease.

3. Fold down the top corner along the dotted lined. Unfold back to the shape in step 1.

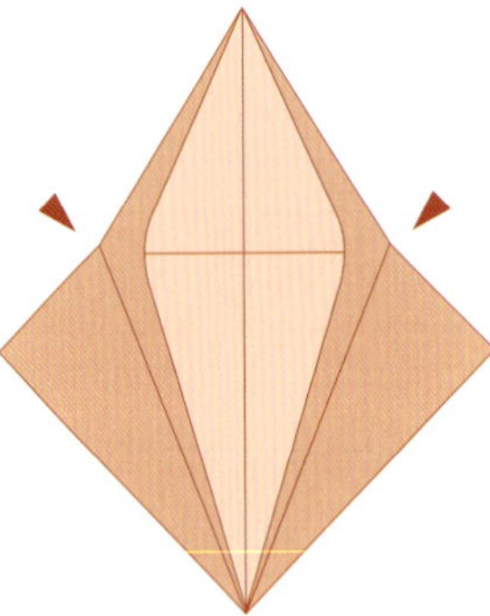

4. Lift the bottom corner to open the top square and fold it along the creases created in steps 2 and 3 and flatten.

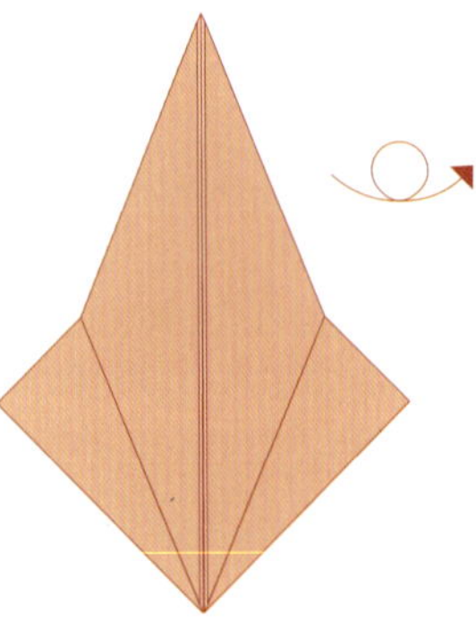

5. Flip the figure over and repeat steps 2, 3 and 4.

Fish Base

- Many origami fish figures begin with this diamond-shaped base.

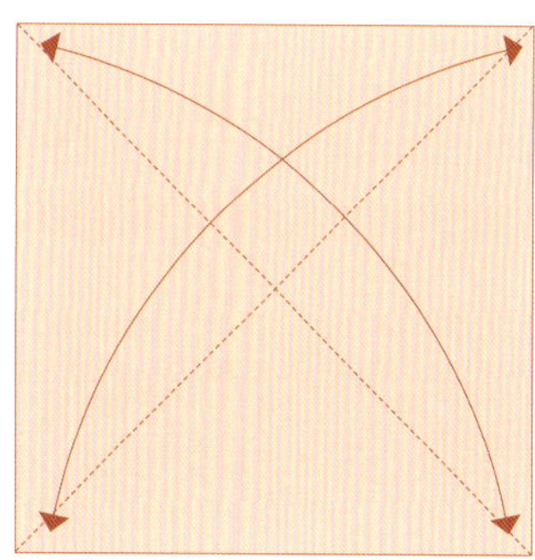

1. Fold the square along the diagonal in both directions and unfold.

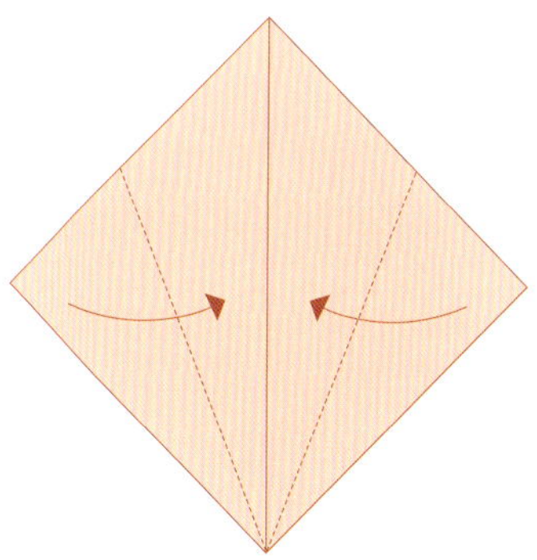

2. Fold in the lower left and right edges of the square to meet along the central fold line. Unfold.

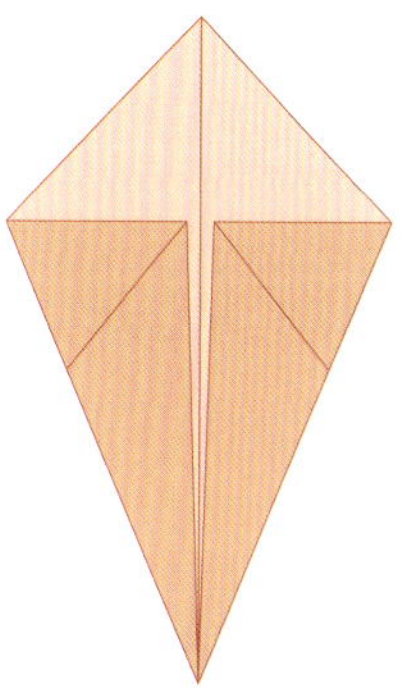

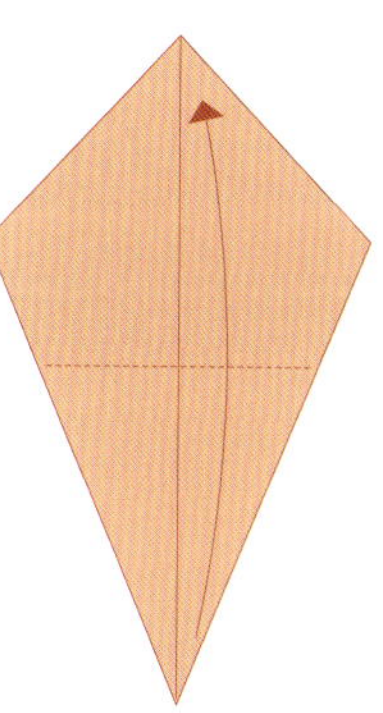

3. Flip it over. Fold the bottom corner to the top corner.

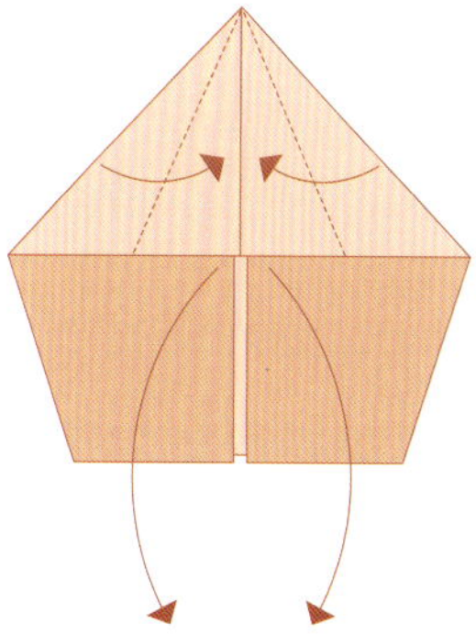

4. Fold the upper right edge to the central crease. Then pull the folded trapezoid out and fold it along the crease. Repeat the step on the left side.

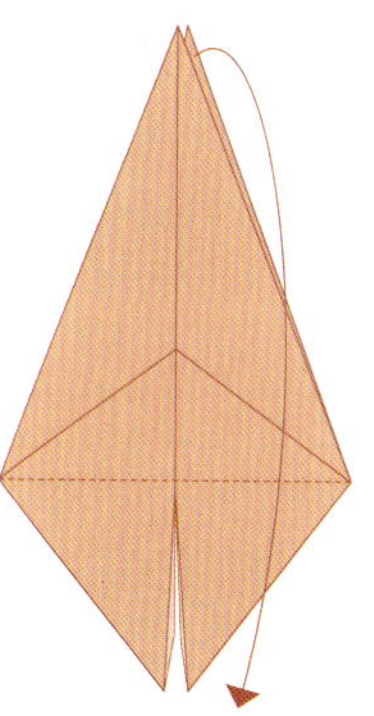

5. Fold the top flap down and turn the figure over.

Tearing

Tearing is a technique of creating paper strips and shapes using only your fingers. Whether done randomly or with control, tearing can produce interesting edges and unexpected, irregular results that work for collage, card making, altered art, and scrapbooking.

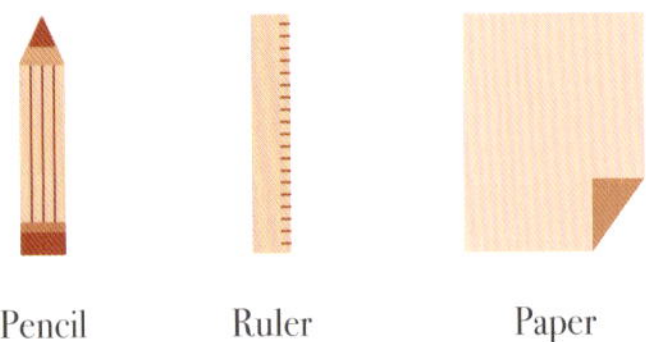

Pencil Ruler Paper

How to Determine the Paper Grain Direction

All mechanically produced paper has a grain, and it is easiest to tear paper parallel to its grain. Tearing against the grain will result in uneven edges. To find the grain, curl the sheet of paper toward its center horizontally, and then vertically, observing the resistance. The direction that offers less resistance is parallel to the grain.

Strips

1. Tearing by hand

Fold an entire sheet of paper into accordion folds, pressing each fold to sharpen the creases. Open the folds out again and tear along the creases.

- Before tearing a sheet of paper, try folding a piece of it into an accordion fold. Uneven creases in the folds will indicate the paper is to thick to work with.

2. Tearing with a ruler

Press the ruler firmly against the crease, and tear the paper along the edge of the ruler. This can produce smooth and exact edges.

Paper Circle

1. Draw a circle and begin to tear along the outline.

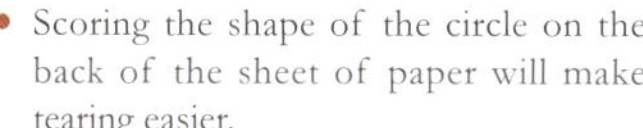

- Scoring the shape of the circle on the back of the sheet of paper will make tearing easier.

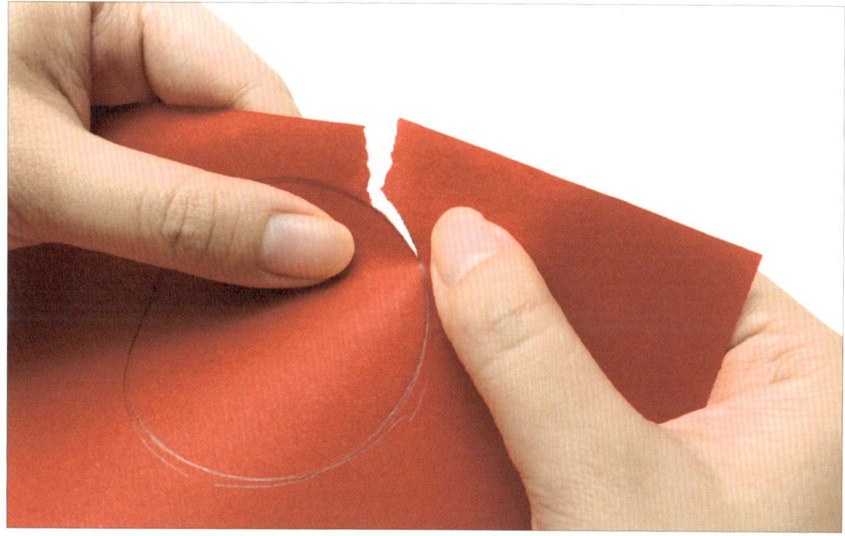

2. Grip the circle with your thumb and index finger of one hand, then use your dominant hand to tear along the edge of the circle, tearing toward yourself. Pause after each small tear and adjust the angle of the paper.

- Tearing paper gently, a short distance at a time will produce the effect of a soft deckeled edge.

Quilling is the technique of curling, pinching, twisting, and gluing paper strips to create intricate and delicate designs. There are two main processes in quilling, which include multiple ways to form quilling shapes.

Quilling Paper

Usually the quilling paper is around 120 grams in weight. Paper that is too heavy or too thin will not lend itself to creating coils with smooth and beautiful outlines. Beginners will find the 3/16 in. and1/8 in. widths easiest to use. Skilled quillers will be able to use the narrow 1/16 in. strips to make exquisite handiworks. 3/8 in. strips are usually used for large works.

Joining Two Strips

Put a tiny dot of glue under the end of the strip, overlap it with the end of another strip. Press the overlapped section firmly for a firm bond.

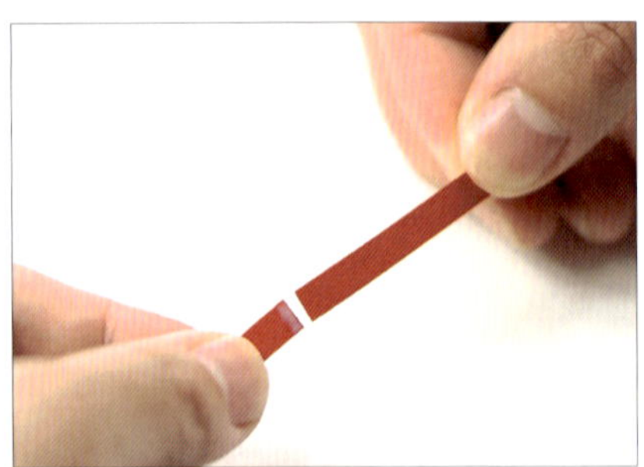

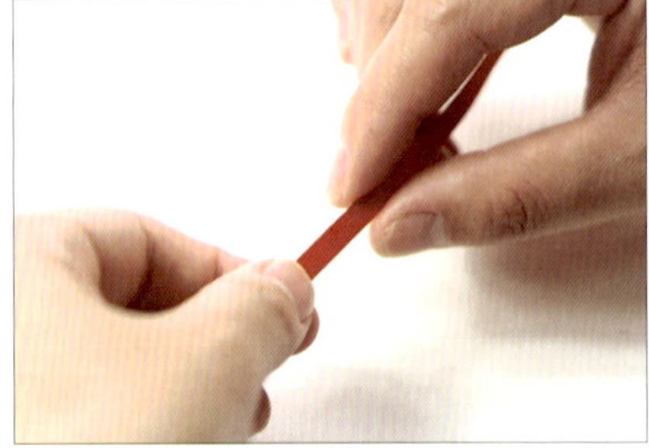

Rolling Coils

1. Prepare a paper strip and place the strip inside the slot at the tip of the slotted tool. Roll the strip with the thumb and index finger evenly with one hand and hold the other end of the paper strip with the other hand.

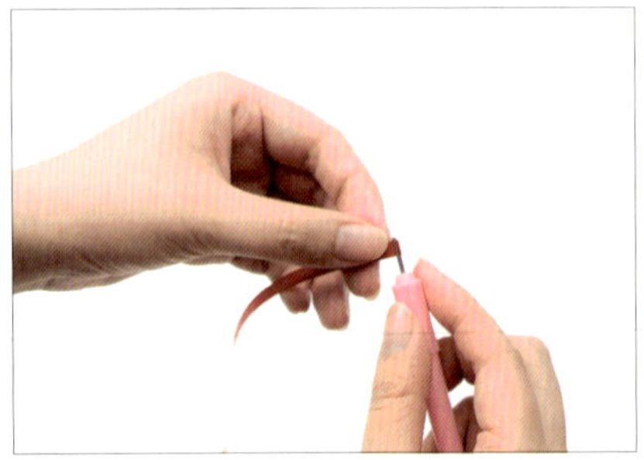

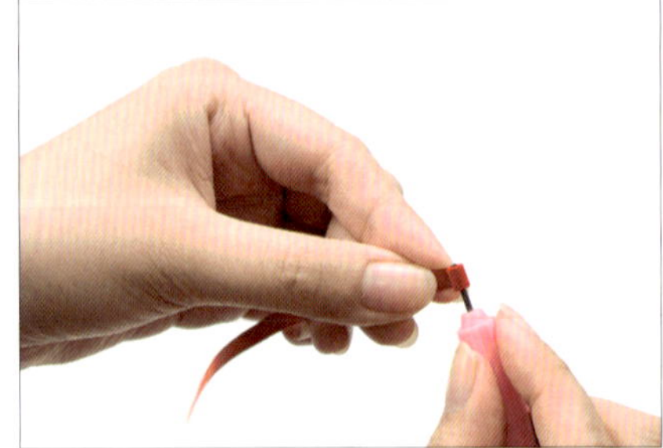

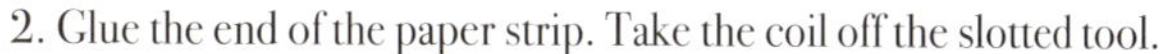

2. Glue the end of the paper strip. Take the coil off the slotted tool.

- If you want to make a loose coil, allow the coil to expand to the desired size before gluing. The coil can be sized by using the circle template board.

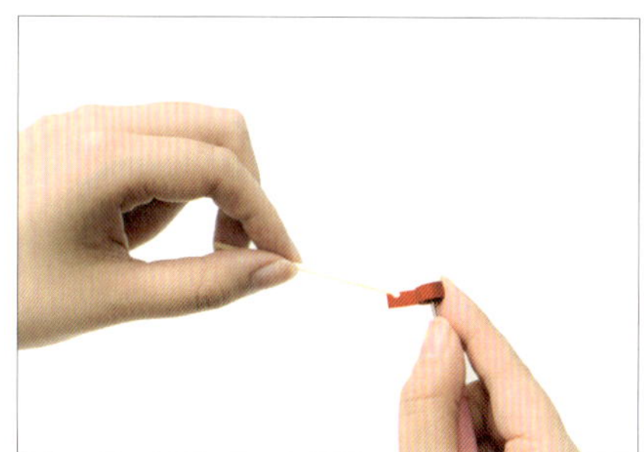

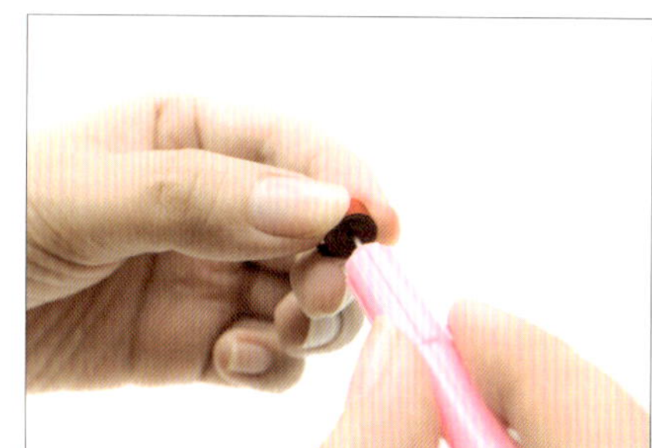

Shaping Coils

Curling and pinching are basic techniques making different shapes from simple coils.

Teardrop

Start with a loose coil, use tweezers to hold the wide end of the teardrop in place, and pinch the opposite side to create the angled teardrop shape. Glue the end of the strip to secure it. The teardrop is complete.

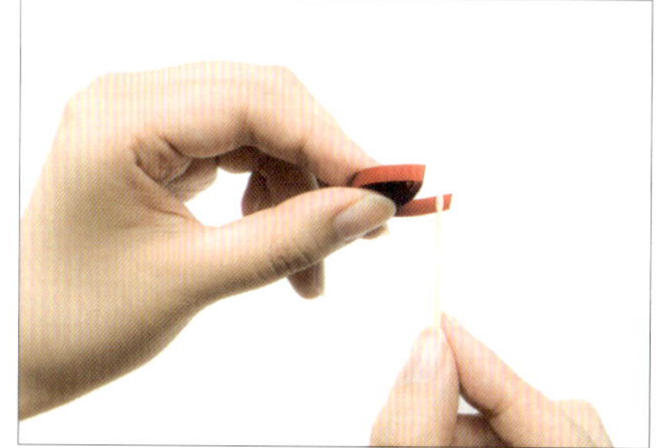

Eye

Start with a loose coil, pinch its opposite sides to create points. Glue the end of the strip.

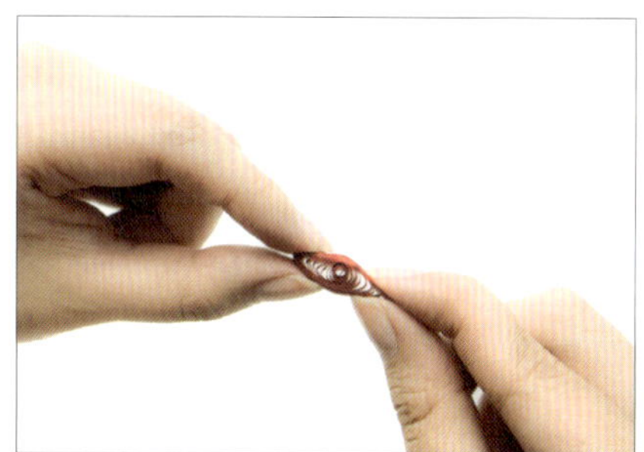

Square

Start with an eye coil, hold the corners of the eye between your fingers and compress the shape. Squeeze the opposite sides of the shape to create two more corners.

Heart

Roll a loose coil and pinch one side into a point. Press the middle of the opposite site with a slotted tool.

S scroll

Fold the strip in half. Use the needle tool to make a gentle roll in each end of the strip in opposite directions. Roll both ends to create an "S".

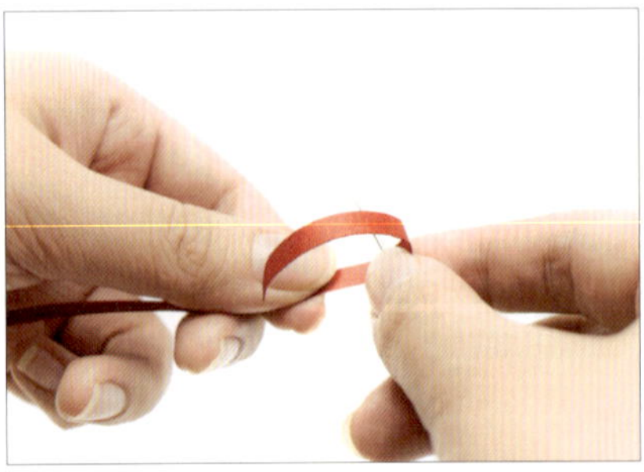

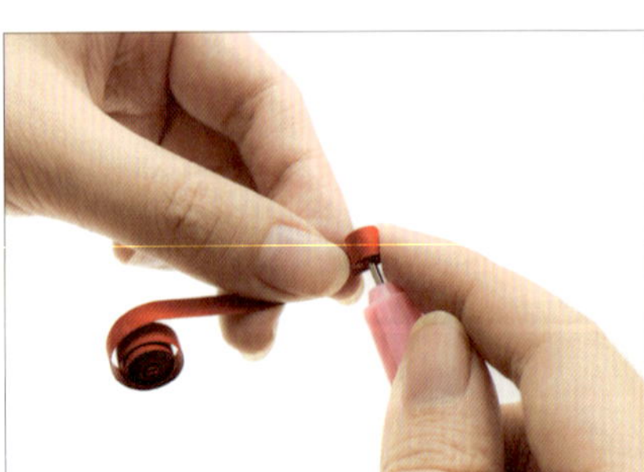

Eccentric teardrop

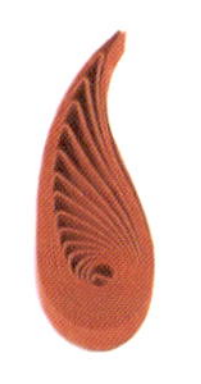
Curved teardrop

Leaf

Crescent

Triangle

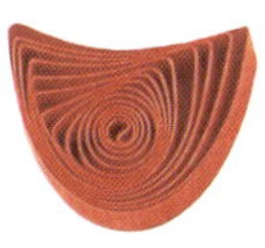
Cat head

Half circle

Diamond

Duck foot

Arrow

Heart scroll

Bud

Cone

Spiral

Ring

Triangle vortex coil

Square vortex coil

Hexagonal vortex coil

Fringed flower

Weaving

Paper weaving involves a set of weaving-related techniques and a wide range of paper strips. It is a flexible technique that will allow you to develop fabulous, imaginative variations from a simple base. Paper weaving has no special requirements for tools, it just requires a fair amount of patience and care.

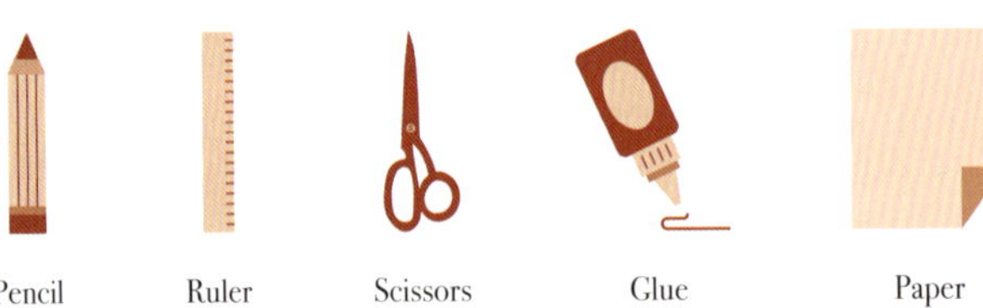

Basic Patterns

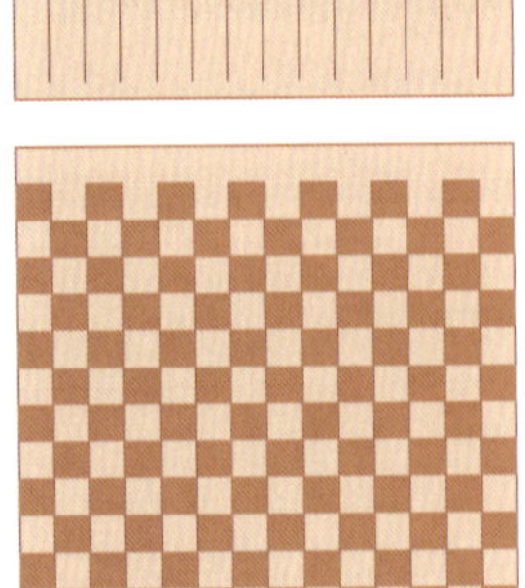

1. Cut the paper into a square.

2. Use a pencil and ruler to draw parallel vertical lines across the square, leaving a 3/8 in. margin all around.

3. Cut slits along each line, preserving the margins.

4. Cut a piece of colored paper into strips the same width as the slits on the paper square.

5. Thread a strip of the colored paper into the square and weave it horizontally, under and over the slits.

6. Push up the woven strip to the top of the square.

7. Take another paper strip and weave it under and over each slit in an alternating pattern.

8. Trim off the excess paper and apply glue at the ends of each paper strip.

The obverse side of the paper

The reverse side of the paper

The final work (untrimmed)

• Fold down the end of the strip to form a triangle shape, making it easier to weave.

• Insert the red strip into the slits at an oblique angle.

Twill Weaving

1. Take a square paper and draw equidistant parallel lines across it with a pencil and ruler.

2. Fold the square paper in half across the parallel lines. Cut slits from the folded edge along the parallel lines, stopping when you get to the top margin.

3. Open the paper.

4. Cut a piece of colored paper into strips the width of the slits in the square.

5. Weave a paper strip over two slits and under the next two. Going over and under the slits until you reach the end. Gently push the strips toward the top to close up the spaces between them.

6. Turn the figure over.

7. Take a third color paper strip. Working diagonally, weave the strip over one slit and under the next two. Continue the alternating pattern by going over two and under two.

8. Weave the rest of strips until the square is full.

9. Trim the excess length off the ends of each paper strip. Apply a dot of glue on the ends of the strips. Glue the woven design into place on a background.

Paper Weaving Patterns

Collage

Collage is created by cutting out, juxtaposing, and gluing paper pieces from materials like newspaper and magazines onto a surface. Collage begins with cutting and gluing, but the decorated surfaces are finished with varnish, paint, or other materials. Creating collage works can be as simple or as complex as you like. Here are some basic instructions to help you become adept at the art.

1. Draw or print the figure on the paper and cut out all parts of the butterfly. With these pieces as templates, cut the shapes from the colored paper.

- Print a butterfly outline drawing on two pieces of paper, one for collaging and the other for cutting.

2. Apply glue to the back of each colored section, and glue it into place. Wipe off excess glue and adjust it further.

- With the help of a toothpick or brush, glue the parts firmly onto the paper.

• Collage template

Sculpturing

Paper sculpture is a complex art form that allows you to transform a flat sheet into a three-dimensional structure with volume, through techniques such as cutting, folding, and pasting. In general, paper sculpture is begun by drawing each part of a design onto a sheet of paper, cutting it out, and then folding and shaping it before the parts are assembled.

- The best paper of sculpting is relatively heavy weight. Choices include Canson Mi-teintes, charcoal paper, watercolor paper, and cardboard.

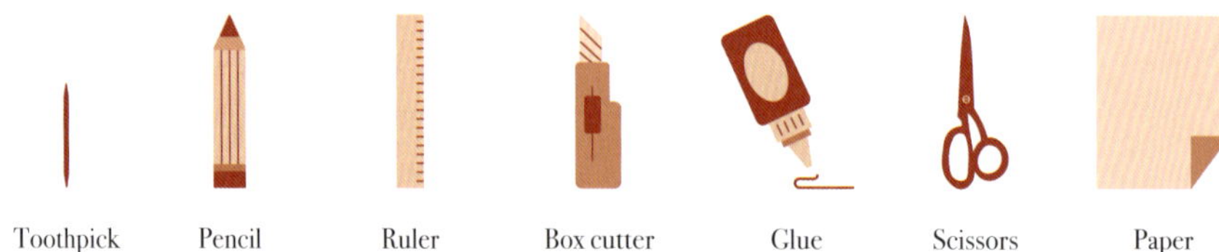

Basic Steps

1. Choose your paper, white or colored as needed.

2. Sketch your design, detailing the shape of each section from a three-dimensional point of view. Measure the design and mark the pasting positions. Alternatively you can print out a design from the Internet, attach it to your sheet of paper with tape or paperclips, and proceed to cutting out the design.

- Mark each part of the design so you will know how they fit together on the paper.

3. Cut out each shape of the design using an X-Acto knife or scissors.

- A ruler can be used as a guide to draw straight lines.

4. Precision folding is of prime importance to paper sculpture. In order to achieve that precision, you will need to score each fold line with a engraving pen, the back of a box cutter or the edge of a bone folder before making the fold. Apply minimal pressure as you make the score to avoid cutting through the paper.

- A cutting mat can help to protect your desk from cutting.

5. Fold the paper along the scored lines, working carefully through the curved sections. A gentle touch is required to create a three-dimensional effect.

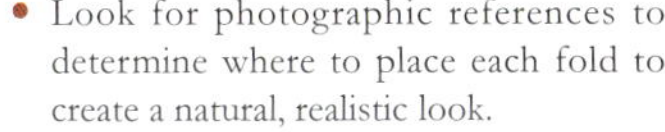

- Look for photographic references to determine where to place each fold to create a natural, realistic look.

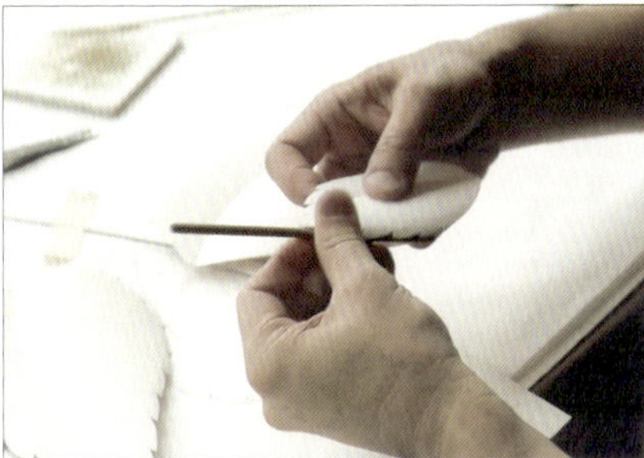

6. Glue the folded parts into place with double-sided tape or white glue. Use a toothpick to apply glue to tight small spaces. Press the bond firmly with tweezers.

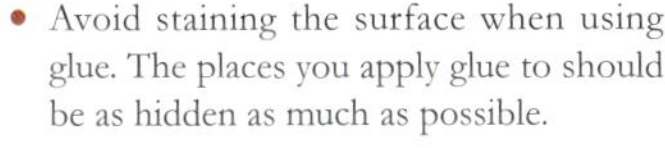

- Avoid staining the surface when using glue. The places you apply glue to should be as hidden as much as possible.

7. Some paper sculptures won't require any support, but for others, a base will prevent the piece from sagging or collapsing when it stands up or is hung on the wall. The support could be a piece of wood, foam board, or cardboard. Attach the piece to the support with glued paper tabs, paste, or string.

Cone

- The size of your circle and the wedge you cut out of it will determine the shape of your cone.

Cut a triangle wedge out of a circle, apply a dot of glue to one edge of the cut, and bring the cut sides of the circle together.

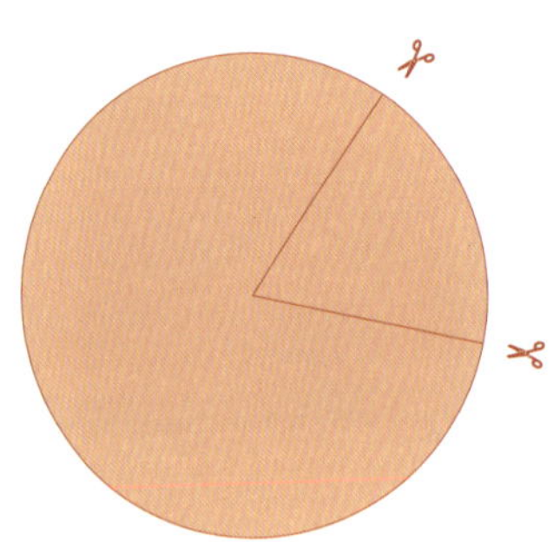

Other Cones

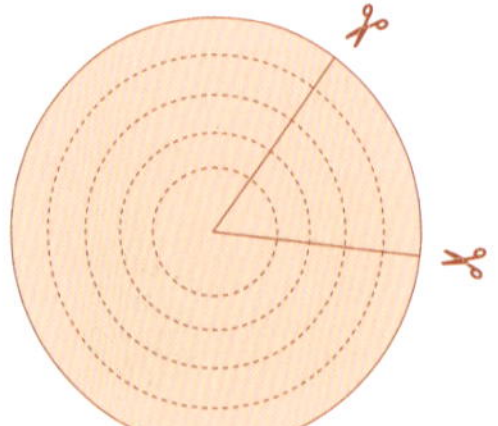

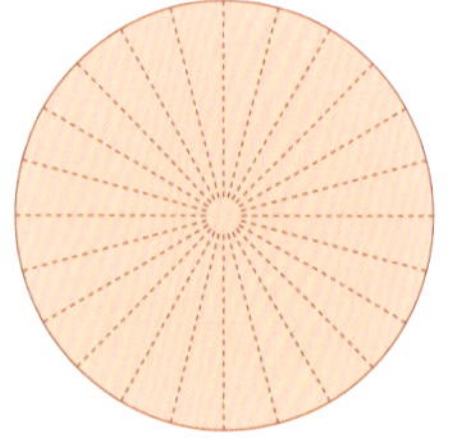

Column

- Leave some space for gluing, which can't be included in the calculation of the column diameter.

Start with a paper rectangle. Roll it, and glue the overlapping edge into place.

Straight Score

Score a straight line, flip the paper over and score a straight line at an interval. Repeat the step over and over until the paper runs out. Fold the paper along the scores and cut the paper diagonally.

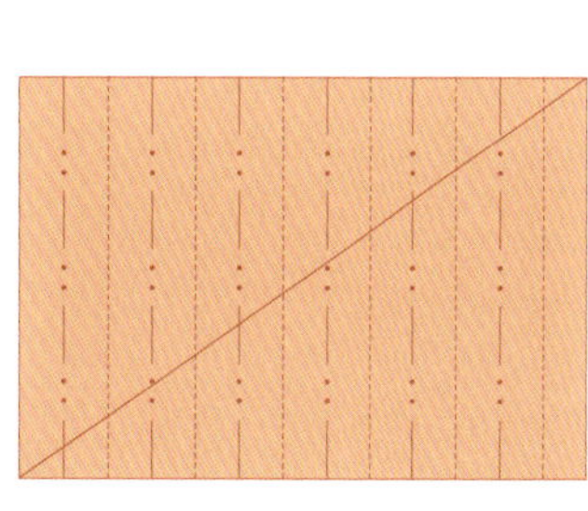

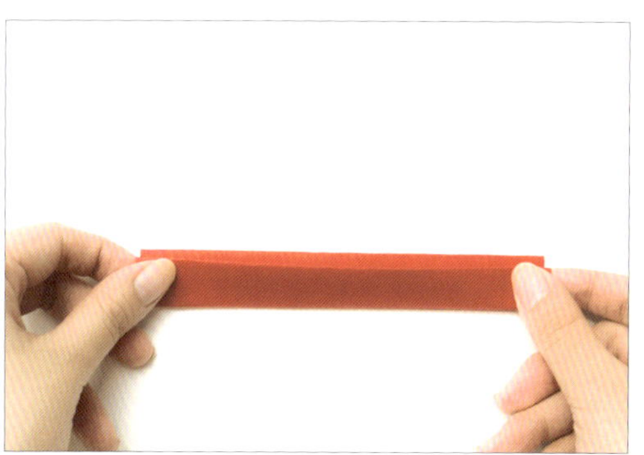

Curved Score

- Do not apply too much pressure as you score, or you will cut through the paper.

Holding the scissors in place, trace three curves with the tip of scissors. Turn the figure over and bend the edges to shape.

Other Curved Scores

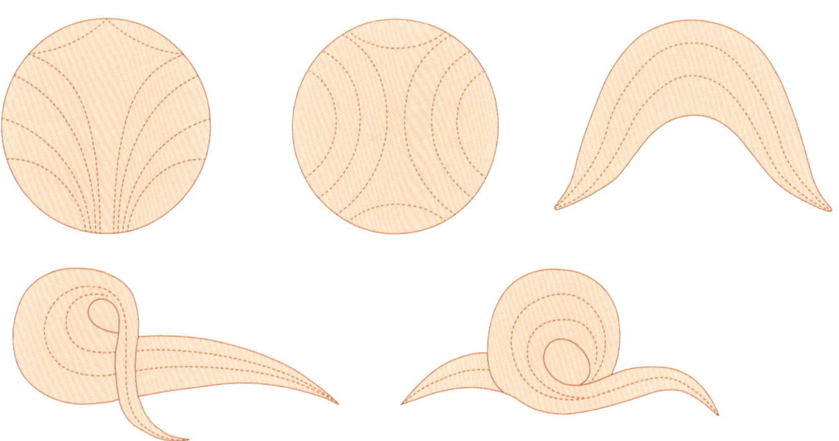

DIALOGUE WITH DESIGNERS

Gail Armstrong is an award winning illustrator working in paper sculpture. With 30 years' experience of working in paper, she never tires of the magic of taking a humble material and finding new ways to create something beautiful from it.

How do you usually find your inspiration?

For my commercial work, I may be given a particular topic, or the art director comes to me with an idea or direction already formed and I take that as my starting point. I find I often work more creatively when I have some constraints to push against, so often a brief that seems quite tight and restricted becomes my most creative work. I then play with my sketches and ideas to make them work as an actual image, changing the viewpoint, playing with scale, color or perspective to create more dynamism or drama.

For the works that I create purely as art, the piece can be a response to a particular type of paper– I have a huge stock of papers that I have accumulated over the years – or offcuts from other works, where negative spaces and interesting juxtapositions occur without planning. Sometimes the concept and art develop from my research into those things. Most often though, they are inspired by natural forms and landscapes; I am specifically attracted to flowing shapes, a particular challenge to achieve when working in paper.

About *Nestle-Love to Share*, what is the difficult part about it? What did you consider when choosing the type of paper?

It was important that that the candy and the bag be conveyed as realistically as possible, so, naturally, the way I made the hands also had to be fairly realistic. This was the first challenge, creating the soft, multi-planed curves of hands, when paper only wants to bend in one direction at a time. I also had to think about what details would define the characteristics of the hands of a male, female, adult, or child.

The second challenge was finding papers in a range of tones within the colors we selected for the backgrounds, so that I had more than just two or three to work with—I discovered that reds were easy and purples were very limited! In this campaign, the color became the key factor in selecting the papers; I often had to compromise on textures I would have liked to use. The depth is achieved through layering the pieces with supports between them and then lighting from the side or above for the photography, to create more dramatic shadows and therefore more depth.

In creating Nestle-Love to Share, you mentioned that you used a number of paper-art techniques including folding, printing, and layering. Which techniques do you find the most difficult to work with during the creative process?

Embossing is tricky because I work from the back of the paper. Even when using a lightbox, I don't always get the embossing in the right place or I raise the surface when I intended to indent it. Some of the embossings are multi-layered, going both in and out.

The most difficult thing for me to achieve is creating soft curves with the illusion that the paper is bending in more than one direction at the same time. Imagine the curves on a sphere—hard to recreate in paper unless you cut and fold the surface.

What do you take into consideration when you create paper artworks for commercial uses, compared with the pieces you create purely as art?

My commercial pieces are generally built to be viewed from one side (the side that will face the camera) whereas my art pieces, even when enclosed in box frames, will be seen from more than one angle. It is something I have to consider carefully when building my art pieces, as I want any supports or the mechanics of how things have been made to be as discreet and hidden as possible. Scale is also something I have to consider carefully, as paper forms can only be made so large, before they start to need support, and only so small before you have to compromise on the detail.

Continuing what you were saying earlier, when you create projects for clients, do you work from your own ideas, or does the entire direction come from the client?

My first drawings are very rough in pencil and paper—what I would call "thumbnail sketches." They are usually small so that I don't get caught up in the detail, but just get a very general idea of what the subject matter will contain and variations on composition. They are usually surrounded by some written notes and arrows, just to make sure they are understandable if I go back to them later or if I need to discuss an idea with the client before I proceed too far with a particular idea.

When I'm drawing the individual elements that make up the drawing as a whole, I start by drawing from my head, but much of the time I then search for visual reference to draw from and refine my initial drawings.

The other thing I am considering when I'm drawing is how the drawing is going to successfully translate into paper sculpture. For the client I will add drop shadows in Photoshop to indicate to them the overall depth of the image. And in general terms my drawings break down into a series of shapes and usually where there is a line, there will be a cut or score on the paper sculpture. So I print out my drawing at a size that is comfortable for me to achieve the detail (a standing figure would be at least 2/3 of an A4 sheet high).

What kind of difficulties you have met when creating your paper projects and how you overcome them?

The challenges lately have been mostly practical, particularly the issues of timing and deadlines. Over the years I have noted that deadlines on projects are becoming shorter and shorter. I put that down to living in a digital age where files can be sent around the world in a matter of minutes and software is so much faster and more sophisticated than it used to be. It does mean that I am often having to turn away exciting projects because the deadline is just impossible to achieve... and I'm a quick worker!

I now work on an iPad Pro for my drawings and that has helped to speed up the drawing stage. I also now employ a digital retoucher to do the boring and time-consuming task of removing the backgrounds from the photos I take of the paper sculpture elements. And I have a Silver Bullet cutting machine, leaving me free to work on other parts of the image.

The other difficulty I have is physical strain. After cutting and creating for hours, I now often suffer from severe neck strain. So, when possible, I take lots of breaks (I set an alarm otherwise I don't notice the time passing!). I also try to overlap different stages (drawing, making, photographing, digitalizing) of each project, so I'm not in the same position all the time. It's a way of working I believe I should have started many years ago! But I guess that's the life of an artist—we are dedicated to our craft!

DIALOGUE WITH

Jeff Nishinaka

Los Angeles native Jeff Nishinaka is a relief paper sculpture artist who has a stunning array of work that—needless to say—can blow you away! Over the years he has found various techniques that allow him to manipulate and bend paper to make these magnificent masterpieces.

Tell us a little about your background and the path that led you to what you're doing now?

I grew up in Los Angeles at a time when it was easy to jump on our bicycles and roam the city; there was far less traffic and far more area where nature was untouched. I think that gave me an appreciation or observing and exploring things the same way I approach art. Observing things as they are and exploring ways of representing them are how I like to work. At first I wanted to be a painter but found that working with something more tactile like gently coaxing paper to do things came more naturally to me. I eventually went to The Art Center College of Design to learn how to draw and paint but that was when paper sculpture found me instead. I didn't have a choice, so I put down my paint brushes and picked up an X-Acto knife.

How long did it take for you to master your technique?

I don't think I'll ever master my technique. After more than 30 years there's still more learning to do, especially how to keep it fresh.

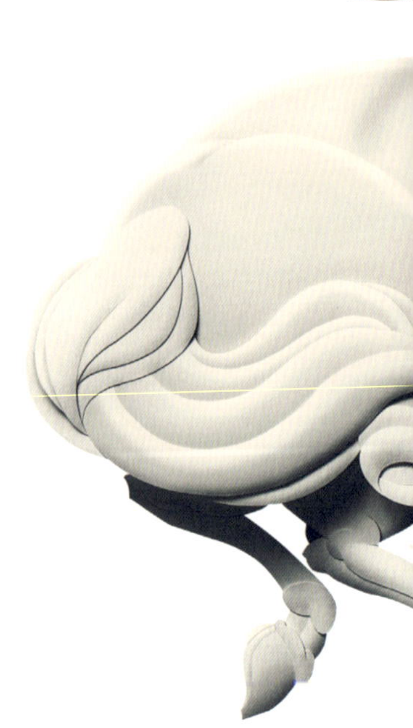

What kind of difficulties you have met when creating your paper projects and how you overcame them?

The main difficulties I have met are dealing with impossible deadlines or high humidity. When deadlines seem impossible I hire one or two assistants to handle tasks that don't need my complete attention or my hands working on it. This includes cutting support material, which won't be seen by the viewer, or simple cut paper shapes that are repeated dozens or even hundreds of times. I can concentrate my time on creating the more important paper sculpture elements that are seen and featured. In situations where humidity is a factor in the dimensional stability of a paper sculpture, I will use the appropriate paper and adhesive glues.

How do you select the paper and tools used in paper projects? Do you have your own standard or requirements for paper choices?

I select the best paper based on the design of the project and its application. If the project is an installation with a lot of large flat surfaces, I use a thicker paper that is dimensionally stable and won't droop or bend due to weight or humidity. If the project is smaller in scale with finer detail and curved surfaces, I use a more flexible paper that will curve and still retain its shape. The tools for all of my projects are always the same.

My own standards are to use only the best paper materials available which means they can be a bit more expensive. Even though most of my installations are in public spaces and therefore only temporary and disposable, I still use the best archival papers available. Quality of design and materials mean everything to me.

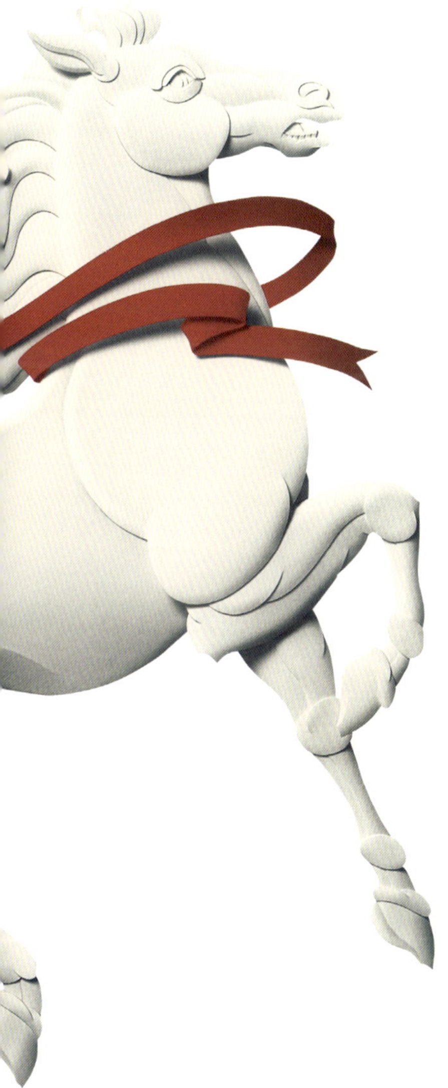

What have been some favorite recent projects/clients/collaborations?

Favorite recent projects have to include the Bulwark 451 video which ended with the burning of a large paper sculpture to the ground. It took about a thousand combined man hours for my team to build and only 6 minutes to burn down. Another favorite project was the Pandora's Box theme paper sculptures for the Iggesund Paperboard Company's Black Box Project. We met in several cities in Europe and in New York for exhibitions and trade shows. A third project was for the Starbuck's 2012 Christmas campaign. I had to make 12 paper sculptures in less than10 days and ship them from L.A. to NYC for a three day photo shoot, which involved combining their actual products with my sculptures. I finished just in time to catch one hour of sleep before taking off for the airport.

Are you involved in any upcoming shows or events? Where and when?

The only upcoming event so far this year is an invitation to visit the Iggesund Paperboard mill in Iggesund, Sweden. They sponsored several events in Italy, Sweden, and Russia last year. A visit this May or June to their mill in Sweden is to celebrate and cap off the Black Box Project I was involved in. We all have hopes of keeping this relationship going for years to come.

What is a source of inspiration for you that is not art/design related?

I box to work out the kinks and gain a fresh perspective. It's one of my ways to reboot my head and open my mind to new ideas.

Who is your favorite new artist?

That's a big question for me. I see so many talented new artists out there. I am in awe and can't say who is my favorite.

If you could collaborate with anyone in this world, dead or alive, who would it be?

If I could, I would absolutely love to collaborate with Tim Burton. His work is so dark and moody, so edgy, so opposite of what I do that I think we'd work together fantastically! That would be a dream! If I could, my second choice would be Walt Disney.

What is the best advice you've ever received?

From my Dad. He said, "Choose one thing and be the best at it. Don't be a jack-of-all-trades, good at everything and great at nothing. " Really, he said that to me while I was an art student.

Is there anything else you would like to share with our viewers?

The only thing I can say is to find that one thing, love it, nurture it, and strive to be the best at it!

DIALOGUE WITH

Diana Beltran Herrera

Diana Beltran Herrera is a designer and artist that aims to repair the relationship between humans and nature in her works by producing elements that are constantly removed, altered, and forgotten. One of her most extensive series is her work with birds, insects, fish, and plants.

Could you introduce us to your cultural background—where you were born and grew up? How did your background lead you to paper art and influence your paper creations?

Working with paper has been not also fun but challenging I can remember making things with paper from the time I was very small–but not just paper. My mother likes to do so many things with her hands. She will sew, paint, draw, and she is often busy in her room creating things for us or for the house. This is how I got started making things. I used to sit beside her and try to create something, making good use of the leftover bits of her materials. I used to make things for myself and also decorations.

I learned from my mother that it's possible to create and transform materials in a relatively easy way, and that became a really important part of my childhood. I didn't play much outdoors with the kids, but stayed inside the house working on different projects. As a Colombian I grew up in a culture where people make do with what they have around. We have a rich culture in hand crafts that is hundreds of years old. I remember going to the gold museum in Bogota and admiring the intricate, beautiful works made out of gold that told me about everyday things and rituals. Beyond Bogota, almost anywhere you go in Colombia you will see people transforming materials. I didn't come from a family of artists, but I come from a beautiful country where almost every middle-class family has at least one family member who creates, fixes, makes, or invents things. It is a place where there is still a lot of hand labor as people are constantly transforming everyday materials into amazing things for everyday use.

This is the reason why among the many materials that I have tried, I developed an interest in paper. I used it so much at school and I learned that I could do anything with it. My mother used a lot of cardboard templates in her work, and that gave me the idea that it was a good material for trying out ideas that could potentially become something in the future.

I feel like I am mid-way toward both. On the one hand I'm experimenting, and on the other, I am constantly reflecting and recording thoughts and ideas.

How do you usually find your inspiration?

My creative process starts when there is something I feel intrigued about and I would like to get to know closely. It can start with birds, plants, animals, or everyday objects. I sit at my computer or look at books for hours, finding images that relate to what I want to represent. I will do drawings to get the right measurements and I also develop color scales to get the tones right.

So many of your works include birds. Why are you so fascinated by brids?

A few years ago my mother got some birds as pets. I've always loved birds, and it made me sad to see hers locked in a cage. In Colombia, as in many other countries, keeping birds as pets is quite common. I think maybe now that will change with our generation. Making birds out of paper came to me as a way to relate to something I have always loved. Through sitting and spending hours looking at images of different birds, of their size, shape, and their natural habitats, I have learned a lot. I have been making birds out of paper for more than four years among other projects. Replicating aspects of nature in paper brings me closer to those things.

What do you consider when choosing paper and tools for making paper sculpture?

With time I have learned to choose the right type of paper. It isn't just a piece of cardstock; there is so much variety. I particularly like to work with papers that are 160gr and my favorite brands are Canson, Murano, Fabriano. I like these papers because they have such lovely colors and they retain their colors for a long time, which allows the work to remain in great condition. I usually cut with a blade or scissors, and have gradually found beautiful, useful tools for improving each phase of my work. I use a lot of glue and work with so many layers and small pieces that allow me to get texture and detail.

What do you take into consideration when you create paper artworks for commercial application, compared with pieces created as art?

When I started doing paper sculptures it was very personal, I wasn't expecting anything to happen but was truly enjoying the process of seeing how a simple piece of paper could become something with a structure and volume. I was amazed by paper's ability to be so fragile but yet strong when you glue it together. I received really good feedback and that motivated me to create more day by day. Once people started to notice my work I started to receive enquiries for commissions, some were personal and others commercial. I really like working for both because commercial works are full of challenges such as deadlines, big spaces to fill, or requests for things I have never made before. I appreciate the fact that my clients believe in me and allow me to put my creative ideas into each project. Sometimes I get terribly anxious because I don't know what I've gotten myself into, but I have always got out of it in the best way and left a good impression. I like to work because I grow and become more skillful every day, and being able to help people realize their ideas is very important to me.

What do you want to say to other paper artists?

Everything I've learned has been valuable to me and I am always happy to share it, I am happy to support new paper artists that want to approach paper and create with it.

DIALOGUE WITH

Studio Marianne Guély

The Studio Marianne Guély is a team of artists, artisans, and designers who work together to think through, realize, and produce some unique and magical projects. They have developed a wonderful expertise and a decidedly French savoir-faire.

Could you introduce to us your background and what kind of artistic influences that affect you the most? Are these things reflected in your works?

I was surrounded by a family of avid readers, and grew up in a home filled with books as well as beautiful textiles. The feel, touch, and even the scent of these materials are very much tied to my childhood in Normandy. The setting was almost fairy tale-like – a château dating back to the XVII century and above all, a beautiful garden filled with a large variety of flowers and foliage where I spent a lot of time, day dreaming. That garden has clearly influenced many of the floral and vegetal-inspired works that I have done. This atmosphere also instilled in me a profound appreciation for my country's history, culture, and traditions, which I often draw upon to create each unique atmosphere or universe. I also love to travel, so vacations to exotic destinations or to places that have a particular ambiance have an impact on my work as well.

Where does your inspiration come from in terms of different projects respectively?

If you visit my studio, you will see that the paper that I use and that inspires me is sourced from around the world–all over Europe, Japan, Korea, other countries. Each paper that I use is chosen specifically for each individual project. It can begin simply with just drawing on a piece of paper and with a scalpel or blade in hand. My method is similar to how one would approach calligraphy except I am holding a blade rather than a brush. In addition to traditional methods, there are also techniques such as micro-perforation, laser cutting, and digital cutting that are used to achieve the very different desired effects.

What is the best thing that you have discovered from creating with paper?

Every day is different as is every commission. So it is always a challenge to imagine new projects, find the appetite to create something different, and make each proposal unique, giving it both identity and integrity.

On the other hand, just this morning what was supposed to be a relatively simple magazine photo shoot with a background of twenty paper flowers, ended up on a much grander scale than initially imagined. It's satisfying to be able to listen to your fellow collaborators and work with them to achieve the desired outcome.

What are the crucial aspects to consider in creating for installations of window displays, compared to creating art pieces?

There are no limits to pure artwork and the endless possibilities that I can imagine.

However, creating an installation or window display is an adventure with the client. It is an exercise in listening. You take into consideration their ideas, needs, and expectations while adapting that vision to the dimensions of the given space and the working properties of paper.

How do you think of paper art?

For me, paper is life. It embodies so many things. It is sensitive, natural, organic, and spontaneous and actually gives great acoustics too. Its sensitivity makes it also very complimentary to digital work. I love that paper art can be miniscule, precious, and held in the palm of your hand, and that it can be grand and monumental.

CHANDON

INSPIRATIONAL PAPERCRAFT DESIGNS

Duty Free Shop Premium Luxury Campaign

Designer: Jeff Nishinaka

A World of Exceptional Style

T

GALLERIA

SUN PLAZA

DFS

FASHION & ACCESSORIES • BEAUTY & FRAGRANCES
WATCHES & JEWELRY • WINES & SPIRITS

DFS.COM

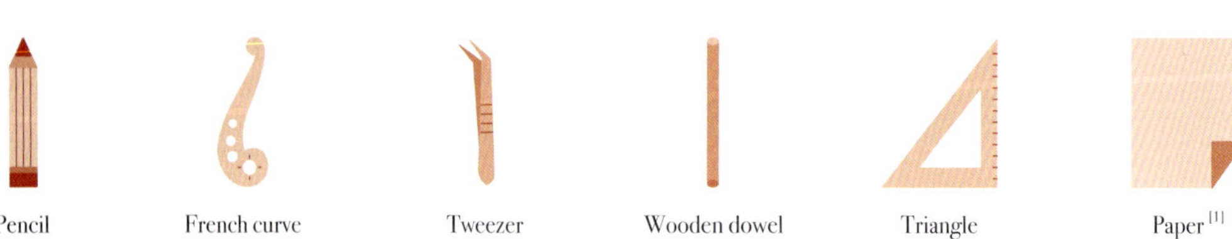

This duty-free shop premium luxury campaign was aimed at raising awareness of T Galleria as a global premium luxury dealer. This handmade project created a series of images including the Dragon Boat, Hong Kong city skyline, paper lanterns, and cherry blossoms to vividly show various aspects of Asian culture and Asian lifestyle.

[1] 3-Ply Strathmore Vellum Paper

A World of Exceptional Style

FASHION & ACCESSORIES • BEAUTY & FRAGRANCES
WATCHES & JEWELRY • WINES & SPIRITS

DFS.COM

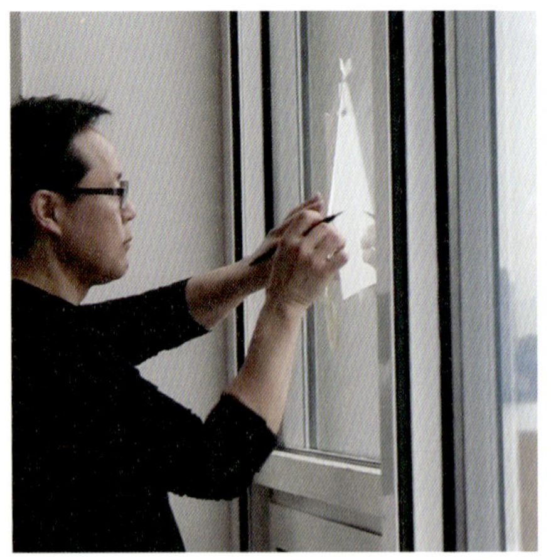

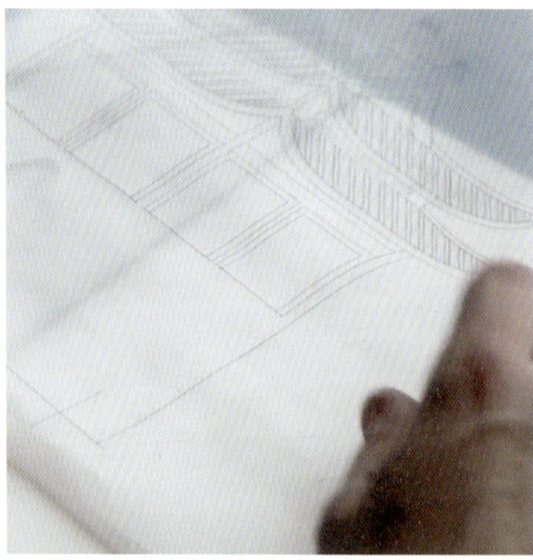

1. Draw the design on carbon paper. Put the paper on a window so that you can see the outline and detail of every figure clearly.

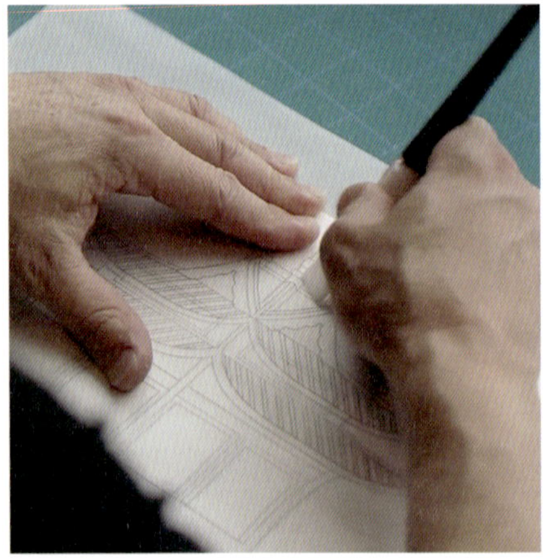

2. Place the carbon paper on a sheet of white cardboard. Rub the back of carbon paper with the smooth end of the pen or another tool to transfer the design onto the cardboard quickly and evenly.

3. Tape down the four corners of the paper prior to cutting it to prevent it from moving. When you cut out curved shapes, you can leave the paper or cardstock taped in place, or pick it up and turn it as you cut.

4. A paper punch is helpful when the work needs many holes. Place a thick cardboard under the white cardboard. Hold the punch vertically on the cardboard and then drill a series of holes with a hammer. As to other cut parts, you can fold them down the middle or curl their edges with a stick to add the sense of three-dimension.

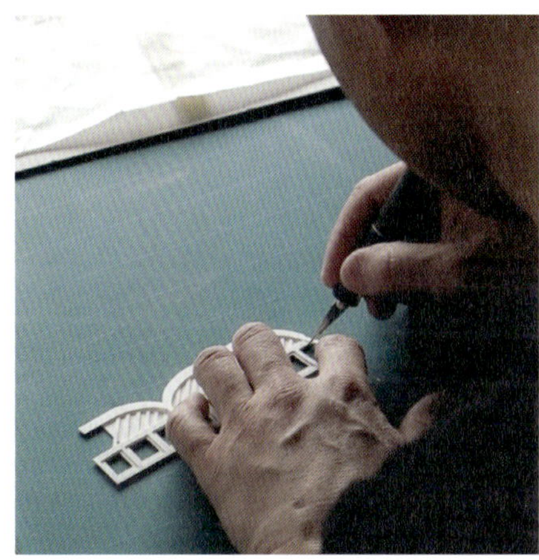

5. Carve out sections of the design as needed. Layer the various elements of each design to determine their positions, then glue them to the framework.

6. Use your finger to spread glue evenly and prevent it from running while you assemble the pieces. A thin dowel can be useful for inserting glue into tight spaces, for instance, when you need to add glue to the space between the parts.

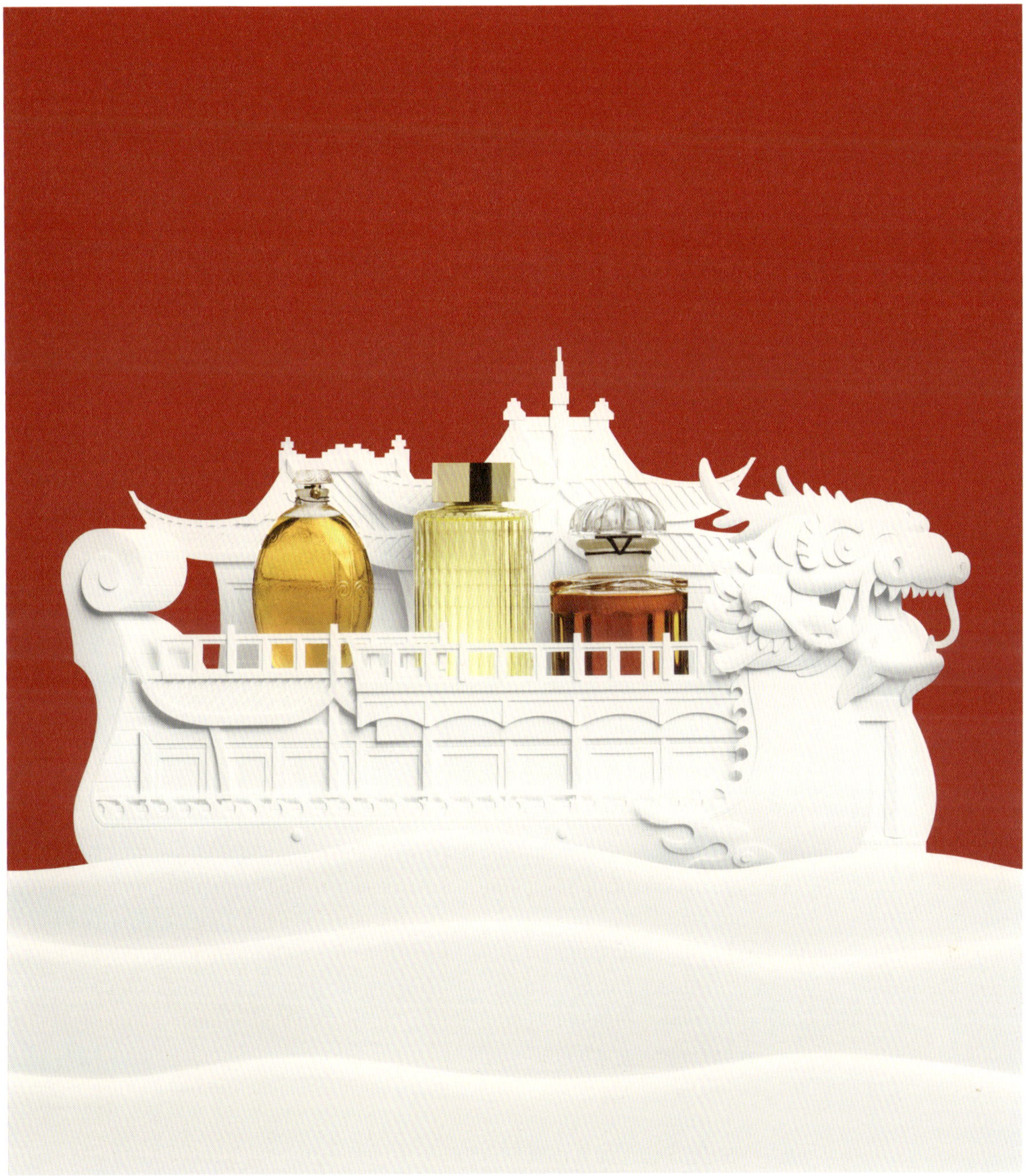

Strasbourg Capitale De Noel

Designer: Sam Pierpoint

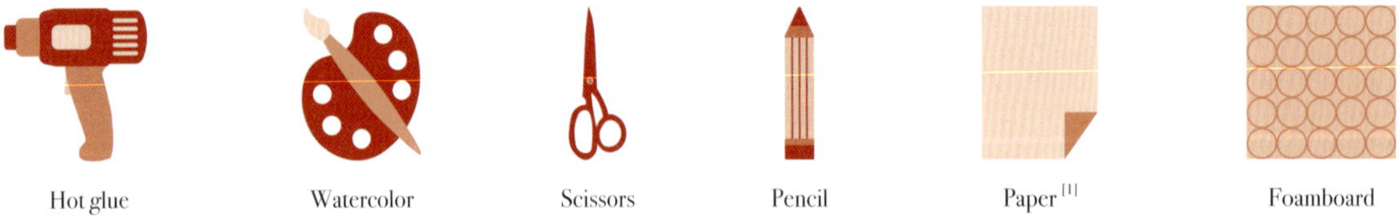

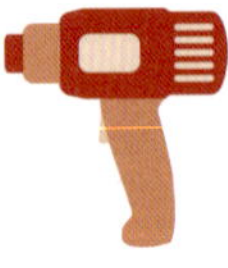
Hot glue

Watercolor

Scissors

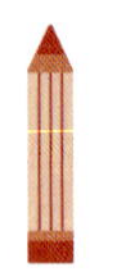
Pencil

Paper [1]

Foamboard

A paper sculpture of the city of Strasbourg was created to launch a successful campaign promoting Strasbourg as an exciting and magical Christmas destination for 2017. With a night time theme, it not only captured the atmosphere of the decorated historical buildings, narrow streets, and canals surrounding the city, but also recreated the ambiance of the city at night, bringing to life Strasbourg's Christmas market in paper form.

[1] G. F Smith paper

1. Start with a thumbnail sketch, and then scan it into the computer and add color. Make the templates of the building and people digitally.

2. Cut out most elements with the cutting machine. Assemble the base by hand.

3. Shape elements of the sculpture by folding and gluing. Before assembling, use a marker to mark the positions for gluing.

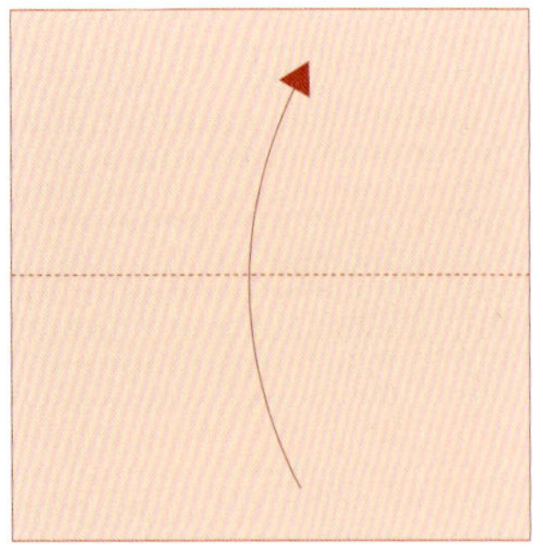

1. Fold the paper in half.

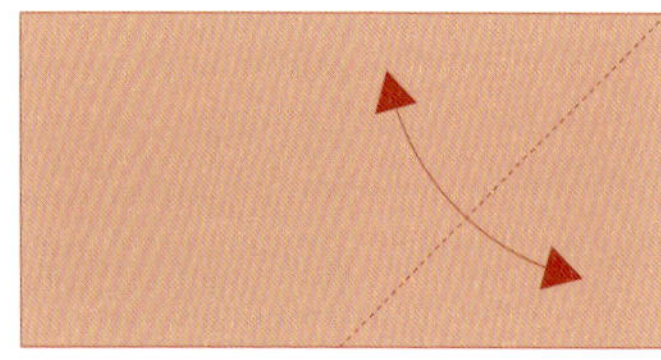

2. Fold the bottom right corner to the top edge and unfold.

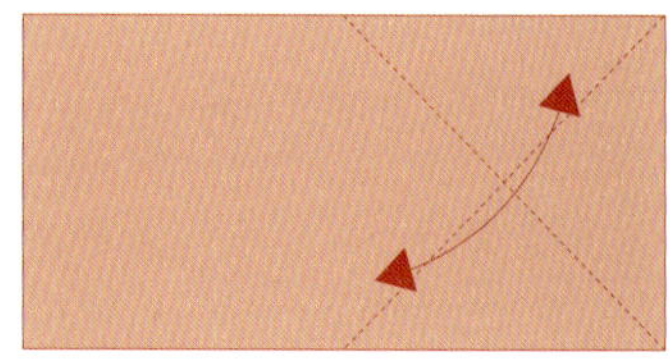

3. Fold the top right corner to the bottom edge and unfold.

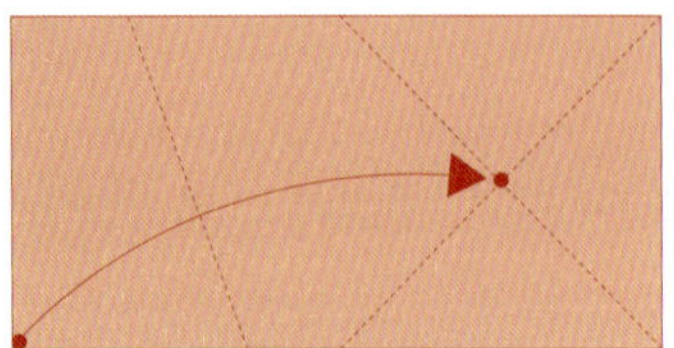

4. Fold so the bottom left corner meets the mark in the center of the right side of the paper.

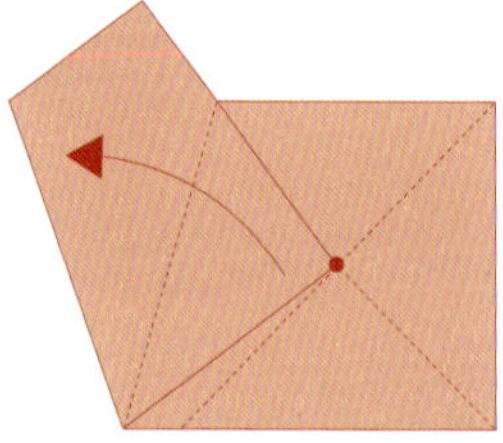

5. Fold the corner to align with the left edge of the left section.

6. Fold the bottom right edge up and to the left, aligning it with the right edge of the left section.

7. Fold the right section behind, along the edge of the left section.

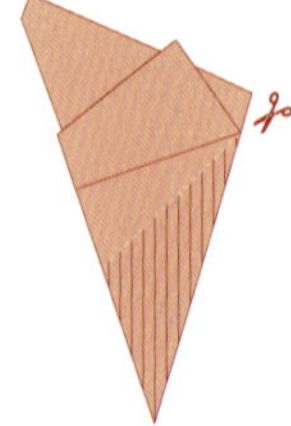

8. Cut off the shaded part.

9. Open the model for a star.

10. Fold the points together, making the folds in between valley folds. Then fold along the points in mountain folds. Open out the model again.

Venus Skies

Designer: Georgie Seccull

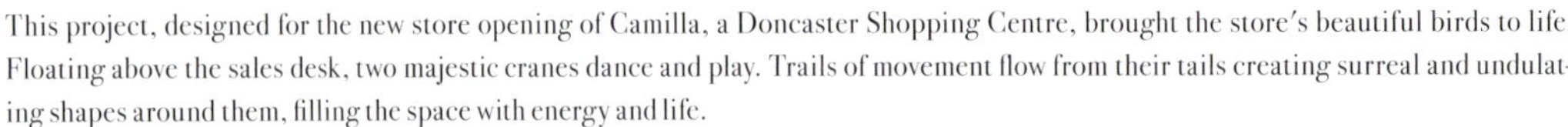

This project, designed for the new store opening of Camilla, a Doncaster Shopping Centre, brought the store's beautiful birds to life. Floating above the sales desk, two majestic cranes dance and play. Trails of movement flow from their tails creating surreal and undulating shapes around them, filling the space with energy and life.

Make a draft of the cranes, with the golden parts indicating the exposed iron wire.

Weld the frames of the bird's body from steel, bend the tail to enhance the sense of motion, and spray the frames gold.

The base is made of the white corflute and tiny cable ties are used to attach the paper to the frame. Bend the feathers inwards to create undulating shapes.

Shiki IRO Series

Designer: Yoshinobu Mizutani

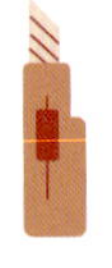
Knife

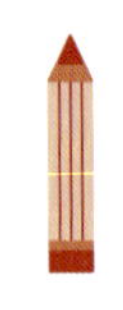
Pencil

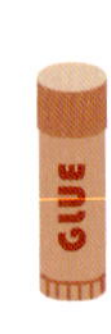

Glue

Roller

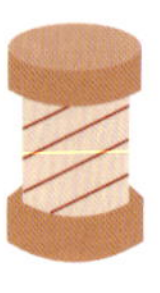
String

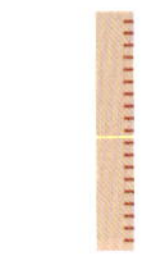
Ruler

Paper [1]

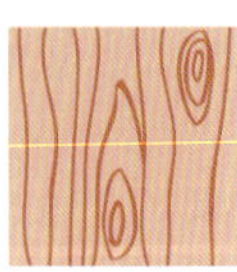
Wood [2]

Shiki IRO Series was a Four Seasons Collection created for decorating modern wall or niche spaces. In Japan, *Shiki* means seasons and IRO means colors. Combined with the backpanel, the products Hana Kusudama added to the brilliance of the spaces. The Shiki IRO Series can soothe people's hearts and lead them into a quiet Zen state of mind in every season. Fastidious Japanese workmanship has given the project a jewel-like quality.

[1] Yamato Washi Paper, Washi Paper, Foreign Paper, [2] Wooden Foundation

• Cut a series of squares in different sizes from the desired paper. Color the cross sections of every square with the same color as the paper.

• After folding each paper flower, thread them together to form a flower ball.

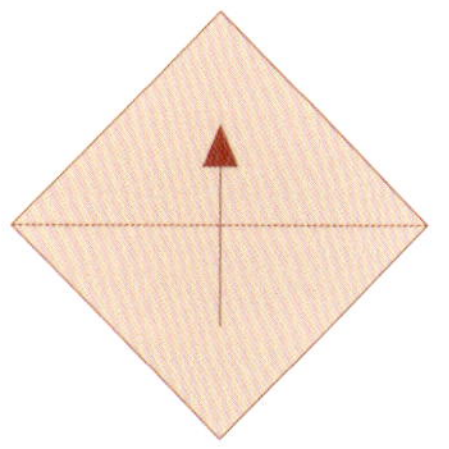

1. Fold a piece of square paper in half.

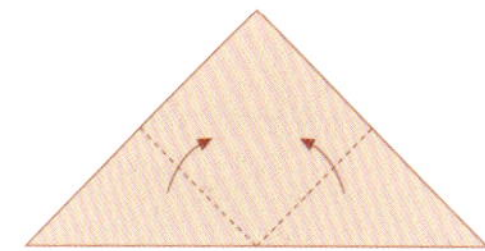

2. Fold the right and left sides up diagonally towards the center.

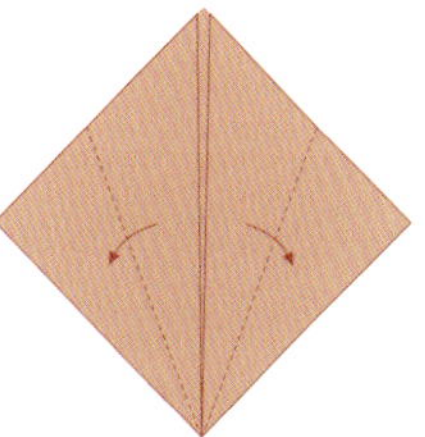

3. Fold the two small triangles made in step 2 along the lines as shown.

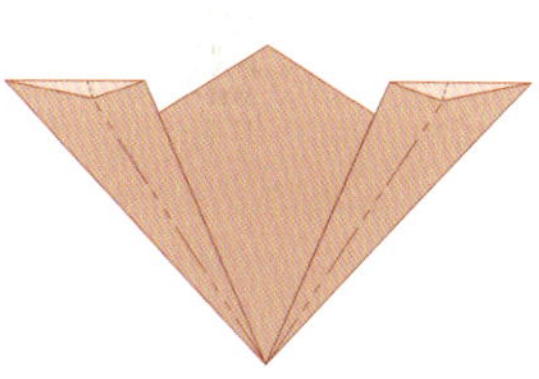

4. Open the two triangles and push them in the direction shown in the picture along the diagonals.

5. Fold the two top triangles down along the lines as shown.

6. Fold the two bottom triangles in half as shown.

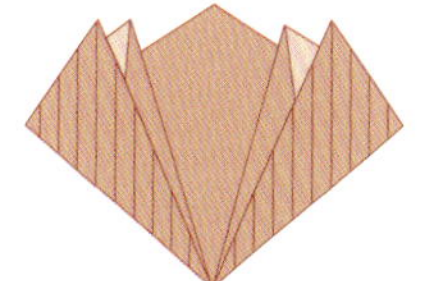

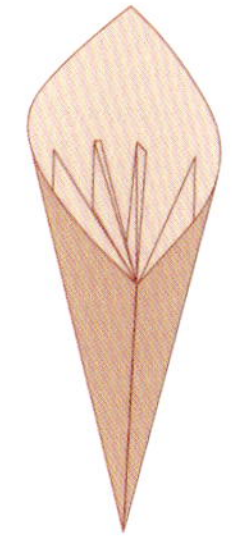

7. Apply glue to the shaded area. One of flower parts is complete. Repeat steps 1-7 to create the remaining flowers.

• The directions for making a petal of the paper flower

Piaget

Designer: Marianne Guély

Paper window displays "Art & Excellence" Piaget was created for the Salon International de la Haute Horlogerie (SIHH) 2016 in Geneva. Roses, feathers, and other decorations were created from craft papers. The particular project was in collaboration with Guépard Agency.

[1] European craft papers, Silver paper, Laser unengraved paper

- Trace the parallel lines and score them as alternating mountain and valley folds to create an accordion pattern.

- Curl the feather with a round stick, then trim it with scissors to create the feathery texture.

- The flower's texture is created from cut layers of corrugated paper. Depth is achieved by layering the petals with colored tissue.

- Attach layers of petals separately by gluing them in the center to create depth and maintain the shape.

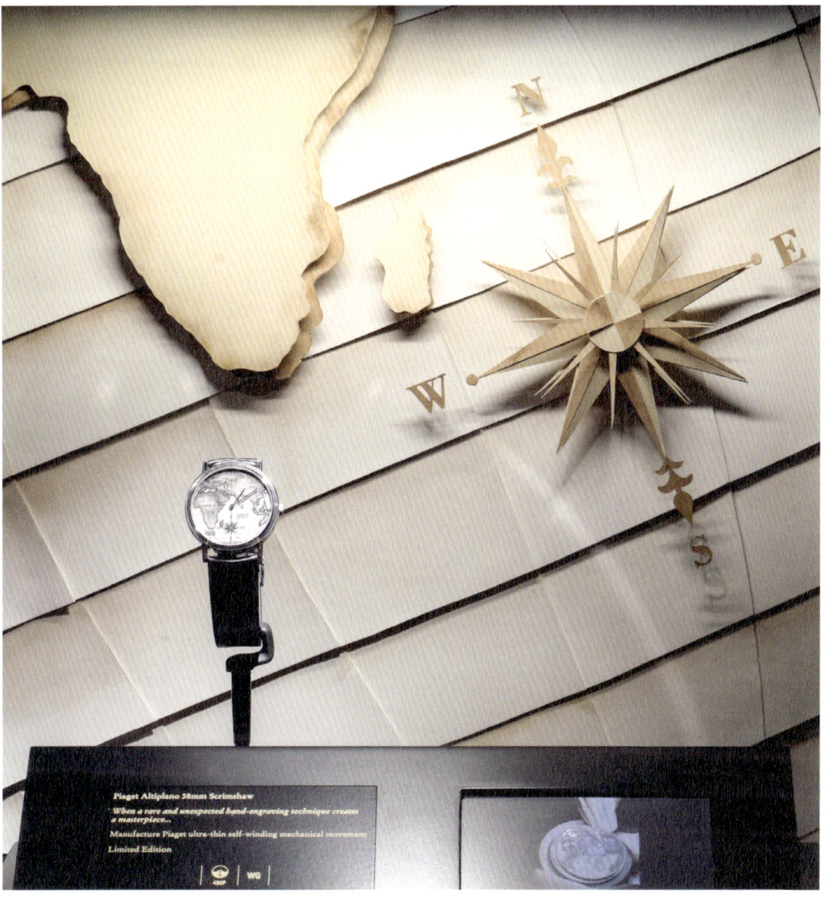

• A laser cutter was used to create smooth, flat, and irregular edges.

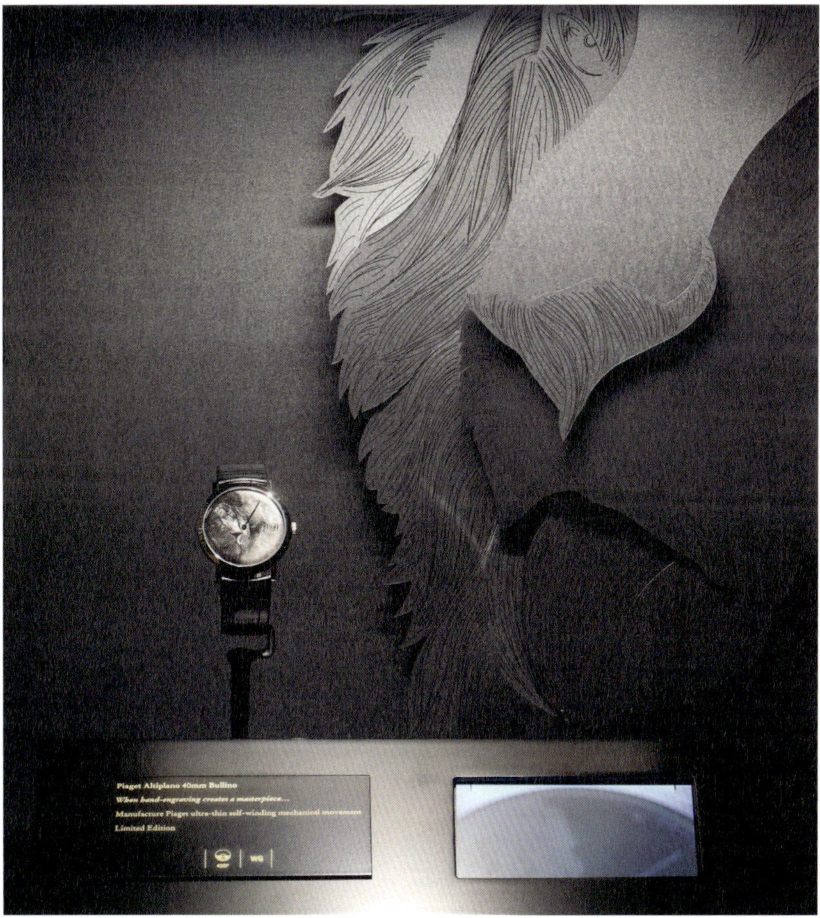

• Cut from the outside inward. The sharper your knife, the cleaner the edges you will create.

Treasures of Nature

Designer: Natalia Pavlova

Glue

Knife

Pen

Scissors

Paper [1]

Cardboard

This project was designed for a promotion of Mousson Atelier Jewelry. All of the visual story lines in the project were created around pieces of jewelry. The models' makeup was kept minimal, in order to focus attention on the colored paper creations drawn from nature.

[1] Colored paper (torchon paper)

- Add graphics on the elements with a black pen. Glue the paper elements together layer by layer, creating a stunning composition.

- Score the paper along the folds with the edge of a knife. Using the edge of the blade will create a clean fold.

Designer: Diana Beltran Herrera

A tribute to birds throughout the world, bird postage stamps are like little windows that open onto unique, detailed views of bird habitats. They portray idealized natural landscapes that never change and resist the ravages of time, closing the distance between humans and nature. The motivation for this project was to expand the possibilities for postage stamps, and create vivid, realistic, and picturesque landscapes.

[1] Daler Rowney Murano (160g), Canson Mi-teintes (160g)

1. Start with a sketch of a bird, drawn by hand or printed from your computer.

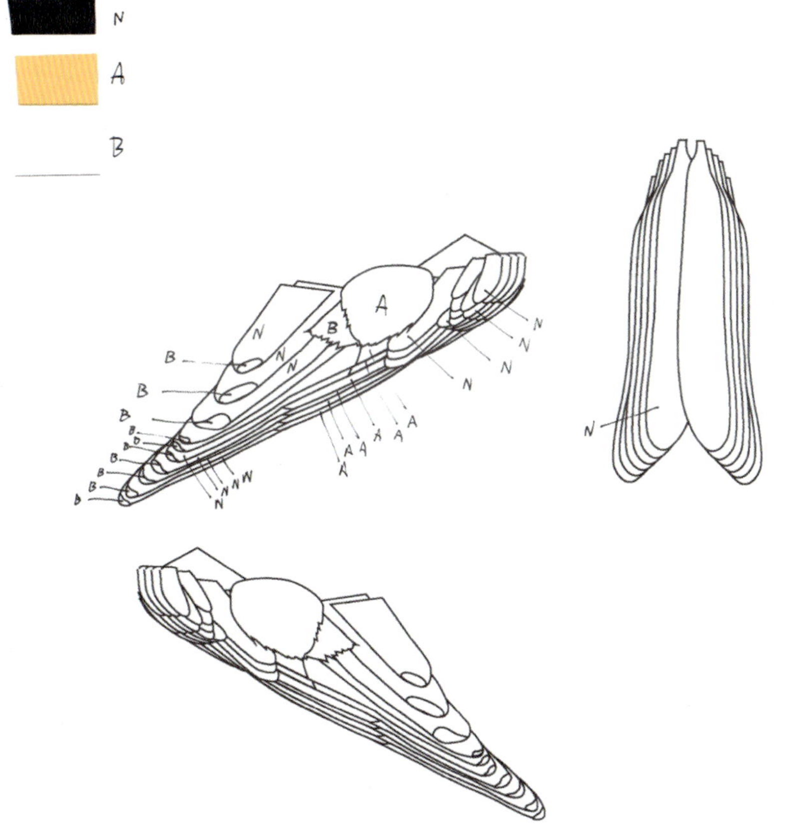

2. Choose the color for every layer of feathers and mark the corresponding positions on the sketch.

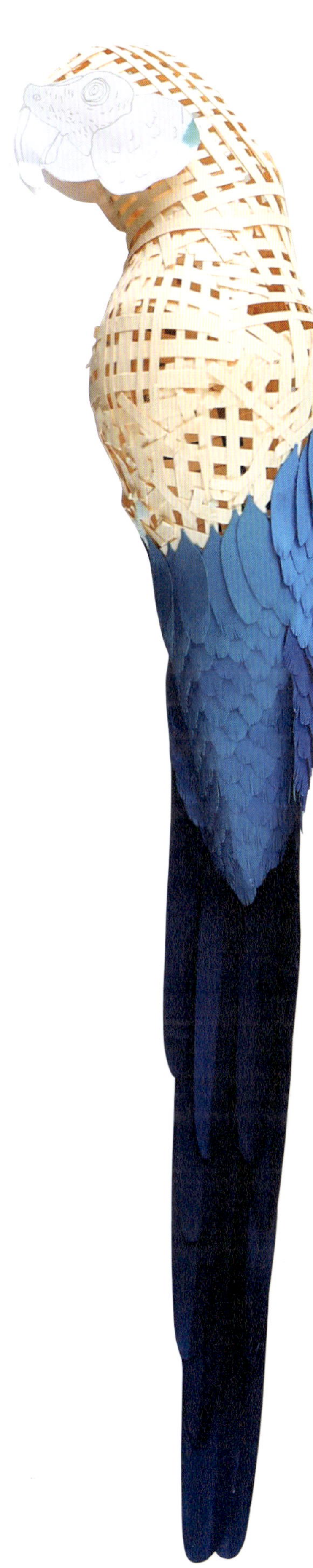

1. Using your colored sketch for reference, define each section of the bird on the skeleton.

2. Adjust the angle and height by lifting one end of the strip carefully to create the aerodynamic shape of the body.

3. Fold each feather in half vertically to make it more three-dimensional.

4. The talons are made of wires and tapes. Wooden sticks can also help to support the body. The designer wrapped the wires with strips, fixed the shapes with glue, and then colored them.

ملسيا
MALAYSIA
50¢
BURONG
KUNYIT BESAR

30E
2012
Cyanistes caeruleus
EURASIAN BLUE TIT
PORTUGAL

15
CENTS
STERNA
SINGAPORE

POSTAGE
Psarisomus dalhousiae
2.75 บาท
BATH
ประเทศไทย THAILAND

The Crane's Gift

Designer: Elena Satsuta

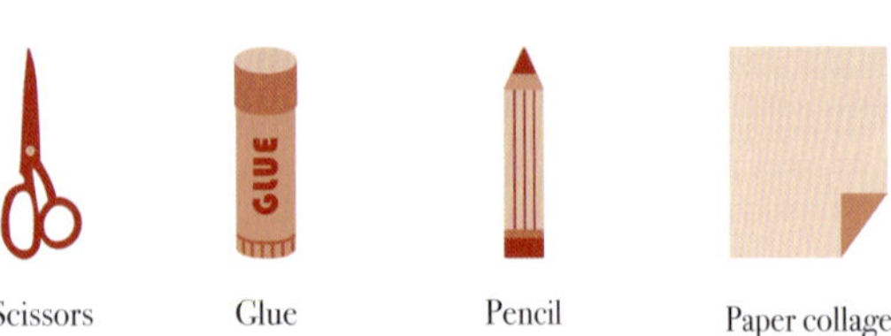

Inspired by Belarusian culture, folklore, costumes, foods, and history, this project illustrates the Belarusian folk tale *The Crane's Gift*, which honors human values. Torn, crumpled paper is an excellent means for capturing an old-fashioned fairy-tale atmosphere.

- *The Crane's Gift* is a Belarusian folk tale. The designer tore crumpled paper by hand to give the illustrations an antique quality.

- Make a frame for the crane and its wings and attach the feathers to it.

- The designer tore paper against its grain to create its ragged edges and add a unique texture to each piece.

INNG DA NAM Music Video

Designer: Val Chen, Ting-An Ho

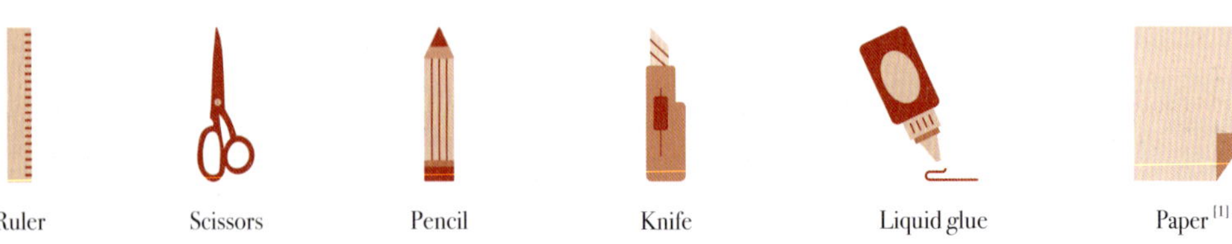

Written by Chinese singer Jing Zhu, "Inng Da Nam"(瑛达適) is a Chinese song dedicated to her grandmother. The song tells the story of a little girl looking for her grandparents in a mysterious fog. To preserve the poetry of the song and present the misty mood, the entire film was shot using illustrations created with origami paper in the Yunnan style. This interpretation connected the story line with scenes, objects, characters, and styles in Yunnan, the singer's home town.

[1] Paper (around 63kg), Tracing Papers (around 27~36kg)

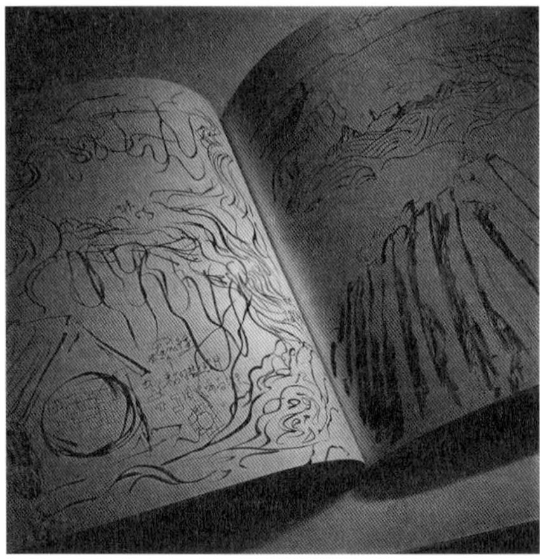
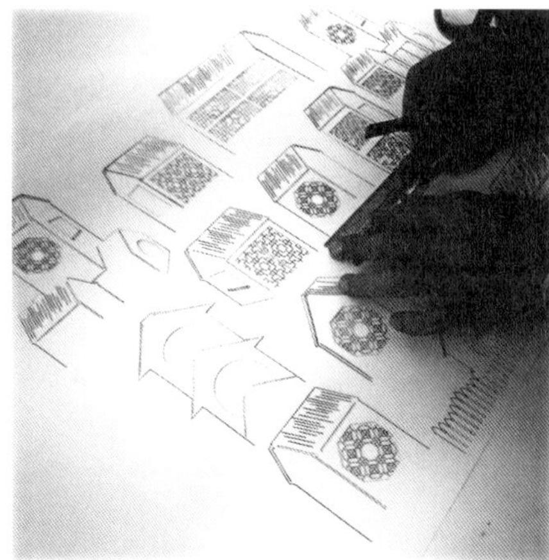

1. Conceive the core concept. Begin a series of paper art tests combined with different origami techniques. Thin white paper is selected to preserve and present the misty mood. Watercolor paper made by Hahnemuhle was chosen because of its stiffness and suitability for paper carving.

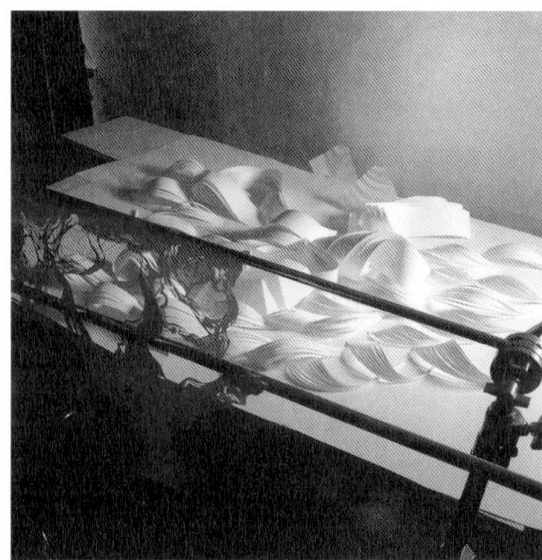

2. Use extra large sheets of paper to create and fold the continuous mountain shapes for the landscape. Cut out shapes for the village from large sheets of paper, and form the forest with layers of silk paper curtains.

3. Have your photography team check the scenes you've created. Sketch out silhouettes of the child actress walking and running. Cut out a myriad of silhouettes to be placed in the scenes you've created. Photograph them in stop motion to animate.

Christmas Pillar

Designer: Lacy Barry

			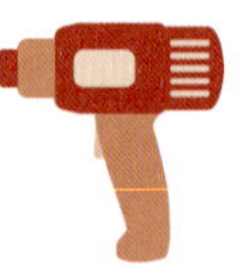		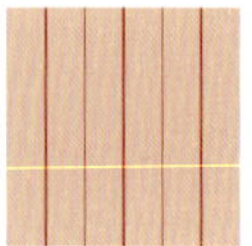	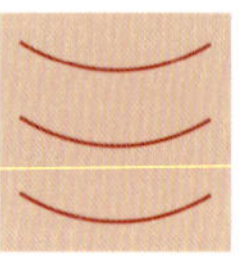
Paper tape	X-acto blades	Scissors	Hot glue	Paper [1]	Recycled cardboard	Paper machè

This large and elaborate Christmas pillar is over 1.5 meters tall. It's lit from within, with the light shining through small cathedral and gingerbread-style windows that evoke childhood memories of seasonal traditions. The pillar's many layers of decoration were created from folded ribbons and paper poinsettias with airbrushed centers. The whole is suspended over a backdrop of oversized ribbons surrounded by tiny hanging gift boxes and toys that suggest surprises waiting inside the Super Store.

[1] Canson paper (around 140-300g)

• Create panels by folding and creasing the horizontal strips into sections of equal size. Create concave and convex sections by curling the paper.

• Cut the paper into a leaf shape. Starting at the tip of the leaf, create a series of consistent and regular folds. Flip the model over, start with a new point, and create a series of folds in the opposite direction, accordion style.

Frédérique Constant

Designer: Mathilde Nivet

Window displays were created for the watch brand Frédérique Constantin Baselworld, at a trade show of the international watch and jewellery industry in Switzerland. The project respected the DNA of the brand and captured the universal appeal of the watch collection. It is a great challenge to create paper characters that are realistic, believable, and not stiff.

[1] Rives Bright White paper

- Score creases on an open sheet of printed paper. Keep the scored side of the paper inside the balloon and fold the flaps for the joins away from the scored lines. Finish all the folds and glue the lines to fix the shapes.

- Create the cuts to represent the edges of the mountains. Score the creases on the back of paper and smooth them with a round stick or the side of a pen.

- Create patterns by scratching the paper's surface with an engraving tool. Bend the flaps upward for a three-dimensional effect.

Make the different parts of the plane and assemble the body.

Crease the paper to form the mountains with natural patterns.

Scoring the paper in different ways creates the effect of ridges in the mountains, and brings out highlights and shadows.

Make the cuts along the outline of the mountains but just part of outlines. Then slightly bend the edges to make the cuts more visible.

Proenza Schouler

Designer: Marianne Guély

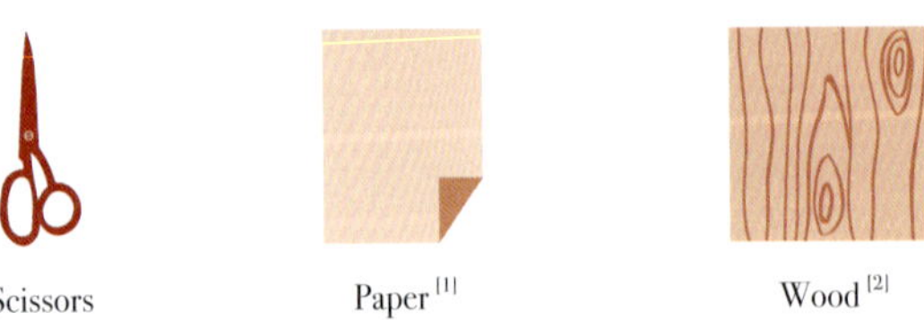

Scissors Paper [1] Wood [2]

This project was a monumental paper installation for Proenza Schouler, Galeries Lafayette Haussmann. Enormous paper cactus flowers were created for the launch of Proenza Schouler's Arizona perfume and were suspended under the Galeries Lafayette cupola.

[1] Non-woven coloured papers tinted by hand, [2] Wooden and metal structure

• The flowers were created from thin and transparent, hand-dyed non-woven paper. The natural light from the windows of the cupola passed through the edges of flowers setting off the transparency.

• The non-woven paper was relatively light weight so that the flowers faced downward naturally when suspended in mid-air.

Andersen Window display

Designer: Edina Németh

Scissors

Hot glue

Laser cutters

Paper [1]

Inspired by the enchanted world of the famous Danish writer Hans Christian Andersen, the artist Edina, together with her talented team, created the new Christmas campaign window display for Libri bookstore in Budapest. The crystal white winter scenery, in which tiny details are carefully elaborated, invites people to get lost for a moment in this world of fairy tales.

[1] White paper from Arctic Munken Polar (300g), Arctic Munken Polar (600g), Glama Basic (110g)

1. Laser-cut different types and thicknesses of paper and carefully arrange and layer them.

2. Remove the masking layers that protect the white surfaces. Create the 3-D volume of the building with an inner structure of paper.

3. Place the layers on top of each other and glue them with double-sided tape or glue gun on the facades of the buildings.

Nike—We Run London

Designer: Federico Galvani

Pencil

Graver

Paper [1]

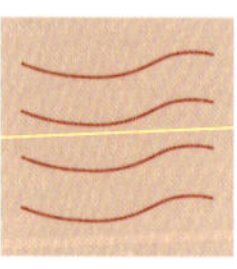
Golden foil

The limited edition invitation Nike–We Run London was designed for the 10k Women Marathon that took place in London on June 21st, 2015. On the invitation, the Nike logo was paired with the special wing logo for the We Run event. Viewed by opening the kirigami invitation, the London skyline absolutely couldn't be mistaken. Nike–We Run London spoke with a passion for minimalism that the designers strongly encouraged and London Agency Exposure really appreciated.

[1] Fedrigoni Materica Gesso paper, folder (180 & 360g)

1. Design each part of the scene on the paper. Mark the positions of folds and paste points. Cut out the shapes.

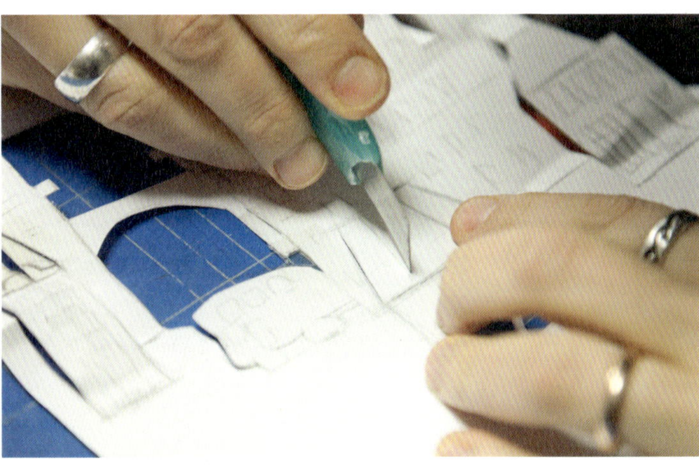

2. Conduct a series of different kinds of tests on the paper. In Tests 2 and 3, the designer fixed the folding issue, but the surfaces were still too flat and uninteresting. In Test 4 the designer improved the skyline, but some parts were too thin and were torn when the project was opened and closed. Test 5 was almost perfect but that was the first test with thick paper and the entire closing mechanism had to be refined. Finally Test 6, taking into account all the previous failures, gave the desired results.

3. Laser cut all the hollowed-out parts you want and apply golden foil to the proper positions.

4. Using the fold lines for reference, hand-mount each kirigami to its cover one by one to see whether it can be pressed down completely or not.

Festival de Las Animas

Designer: Cesar Leal

In an effort to rescue and preserve traditional Mexican culture through the "Day of the Dead" celebration, this team works with the Municipal System of the Arts and Culture of Celaya (SISMACC) to create a new interpretation of the "Walk of the Luminaries." This is a tradition rooted in the neighborhoods of Celaya City. Within the principal concept of the project, the team interprets the transformation of the body into an "anima" or "soul." Elements such as skulls and hearts, are constant themes throughout the visual arts produced for the festival.

1. Make a model using paper and glue. Smear the paper with glue. Let it sit for a few seconds and then tear it into strips. The edges of the paper will become soft and natural were they overlap.

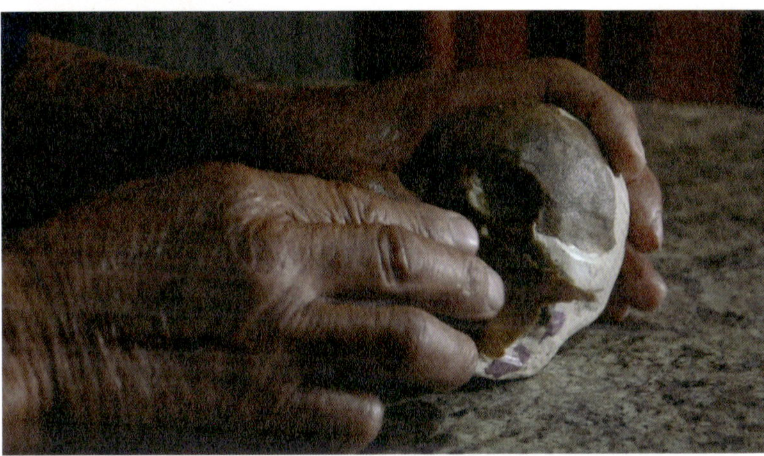

2. Squeeze the strips when layering them to remove small bubbles so that the structure of the model will become firmer.

3. Paste a second layer of paper over the first after it has dried, and repeat the steps. The number of layers will depend on the desired thickness.

4. Color the model with acrylic paint when it is dry.

FESTIVAL DE
LAS ÁNIMAS
2016
Celaya
2015 • 2018
#SISMACCCERCADETI
WWW.CULTURA-CELAYA.COM
FACEBOOK.COM/CULTURACELAYA

FESTIVAL DE
LAS ÁNIMAS
2016
DEL 31 OCTUBRE AL 13 NOVIEMBRE
CELAYA, GTO.
SISTEMA MUNICIPAL de ARTE y CULTURA de CELAYA
Celaya
2015 · 2018
#SISMACCCERCADETI
WWW.CULTURA-CELAYA.COM
FACEBOOK.COM/CULTURACELAYA

Precious Moments

Designer: Davy McGuire, Kristin McGuire

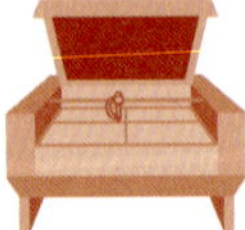

Laser cutters

Paper [1]

This set design in the window of the Mikimoto flagship shore in Ginza, Tokyo, was created to illustrate the importance of precious moments such as engagements, weddings, and celebrations of love that are associated with Mikimoto jewelry. The idea was to create a Parisian style paper diorama, animated by video projections of silhouetted characters who each share precious moments with each-other.

[1] Paper over wooden frame

1. Digitally design the basic three-dimensional structure. Based on the sketch, create a supporting framework of interlocking wooden beams and create a strong underlying structure.

2. Design the facades of the buildings which here were created using Adobe Illustrator. Send the illustrator files to the laser cutter in several layers and assembled on site.

3. Use a green screen to create much of the animation with live actors. The green backgrounds were removed and then the characters were turned into sillhouettes.

Easter Pillars

Designer: Lacy Barry

Paper tape Hot glue X-acto blades Scissors

Paper [1]

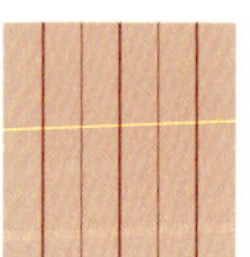

Recycled cardboard

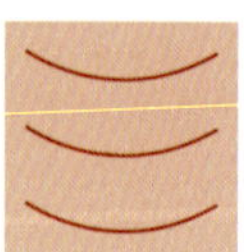

Paper machè

Decorative columns in a Easter window display showcasing Super Store's products. Using palmate leaf shapes, the columns were designed to represent three aspects of Lent: pray, fast, and give. Each column combines different icons associated with Easter: paper palms, decorated eggs, colorful flowers, and greenery, as well as seasonal symbols of spring rebirth and resurrection.

[1] Canson paper (around 140~300g)

Tiger Tiger

Designer: Anna-Wili Highfield

Cut the paper into strips and attach them to the frame.

The frame for the model was made of plywood.

Ragged edges were created by tearing paper against the direction of its grain.

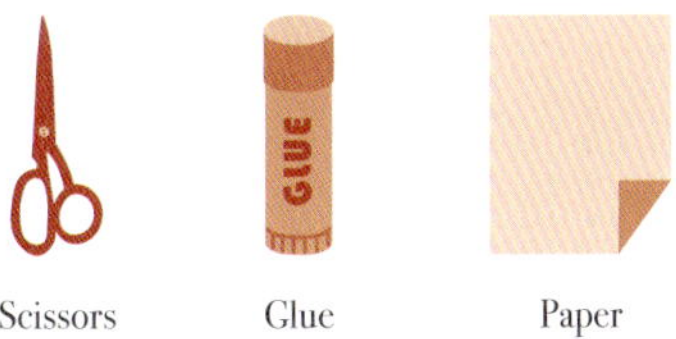

Scissors Glue Paper

The project is aimed to create a moment of vital energy and dynamics, in which the paper Tiger bursts through the paper screen. The title Tiger Tiger comes from the William Blake poem The Tyger.

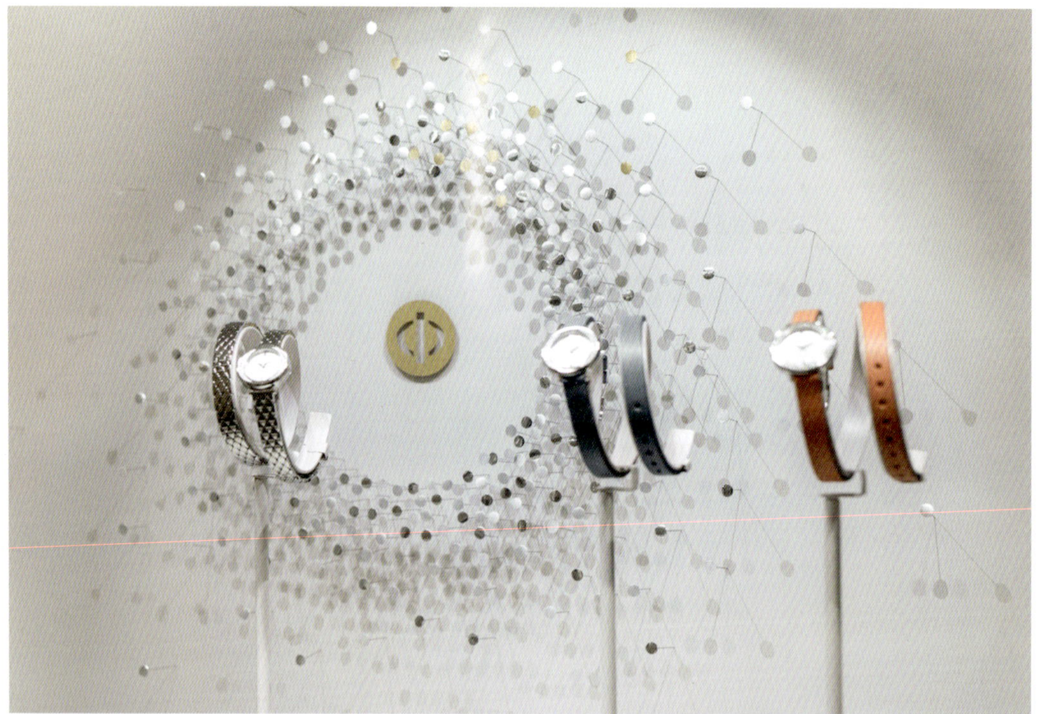

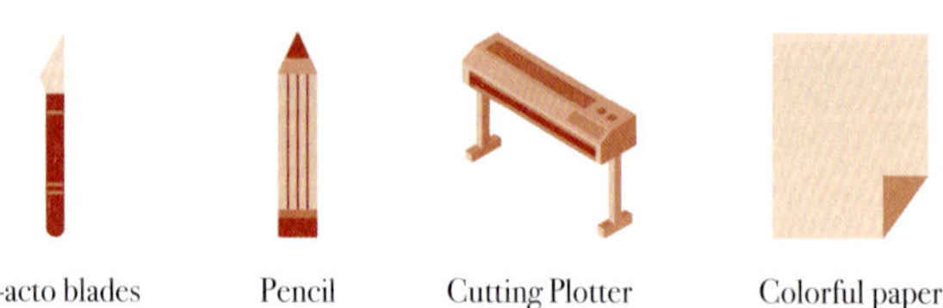

X-acto blades Pencil Cutting Plotter Colorful paper

For the SIHH 2016 show, Baume & Mercier focused on Celebration Moments: happy moments of our lives when we might receive a watch, such as the joyful occasions of births, graduation, engagements, and victories.

• Begin with a small sketch and work it out digitally in Illustrator. Number the different section of the layout and the height of each layer. Then Print out the design, cut and weave different sections of the layout by hand according to their corresponding height. Insert a little foam board pieces between the layers to create a sense of depth and volume.

Regina Maria Private Healthcare Opening

Studio: Razvan Cornici

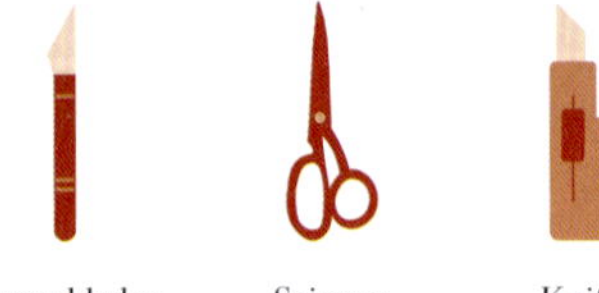

X-acto blades | Scissors | Knife | Glue | Cutting mat | Carbon paper | Paper

This project was created as a visual-identity image for the Regina Maria Healthcare Clinic, which was opening in designer Razvan Cornici's hometown, Timisoara. It befitted the project to have a local designer create the image. The concept was to illustrate the town, including a hint of the clinic. The illustrations are used on products such as pens and mugs, as well as advertisements on trams.

REGINA MARIA
REȚEAUA PRIVATĂ DE SĂNĂTATE
GRIJA STĂ ÎN DETALII
MAI ALES CÂND VINE
VORBA DE SĂNĂTATE
Policlinica Timișoara
REGINA MARIA

REGINA MARIA
GRIJA STĂ ÎN DETALII
REGINA MARIA
GRIJA STĂ ÎN DETALII

British Airways Terminal Film

Studio: A+C Studio

Scissors　Scalpel　Cutting Plotter　Laser cutters　Paper [1]

Gatwick airport's South Terminal, home of British Airways, boasts a five-meter wide screen for all to see as people arrive at the airport for their onward journey. British Airways wanted to use the key site as a guide for travelers of all ages, explaining the check-in procedures. The film is silent, and made as stop-motion animation. Using paper-craft not only generates audience engagement but also makes for compelling story-telling and charming aesthetics.

[1] Canford Paper (300 & 150g)

• Design the airport environments and characters from rich, textured card, including 17 different sets and over 50 paper characters, along with a few aliens and a unicorn for good measure. Determine color palette of the card stock.

• Wide sets were created due to the unique size and ratio of the five-meter British Airways Terminal screen. To work out the correct scale, depth, and dimensions, the sets and props were mocked up in cardboard first for camera testing. The widest set was the airport departure lounge, which came in at nearly 8 feet wide.

THAT'S ONE LESS THING
TO TAKE CARE OF

FOR LONG HAUL FLIGHTS, IT'S 60 MINUTES

BRITISH AIRWAYS

- After the model-making and sets complete, you can begin to shoot the stop motion animation. Ensure everything is lit in camera in order to create real shadows.

• The animators filled, on average, five seconds of footage a day. Move each limb, head and suitcase frame by frame, using a selection of tweezers.

Gates
Toilets

Wondertales House

Designer: Elena Satsuta

Scissors Glue Paper collage

Wondertales House is a book project containing 10 stories that take place in a magic house where ordinary people meet various magic characters. Each story has a "statement" of good deeds.

- The fibers are more apparent in torn handmade paper handmade paper than machine-made paper

- The artwork is made of patterned paper. The thicker it is, the clearer the texture shows.

- Make small cuts at tiny, even intervals on a strip. Roll it in to a flower and glue the end in place.

- Create the dress patterns by scoring.

• Mimicking textures of flowers, the subtle creases give you a sense of fragility.

• Score the details of braided hair. Notice the changes of the light and shadow on it.

Chandon

Studio: REVERBERE studio

This set design and paper art was created as a part of an international Instagram campaign for the LVMH brand Chandon. The series of visuals was made for the launch of a new range of sparkling white and rosé wine. Aiming at the millennial generation, the paper set design evoked an uninhibited good life with a fresh and colorful universe, inviting people to share a cold glass and relax.

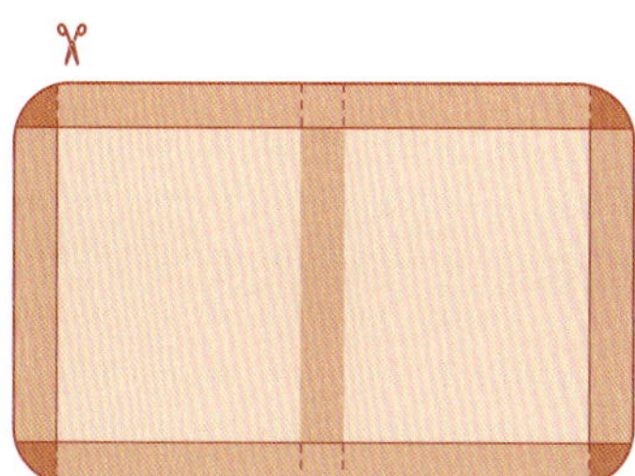

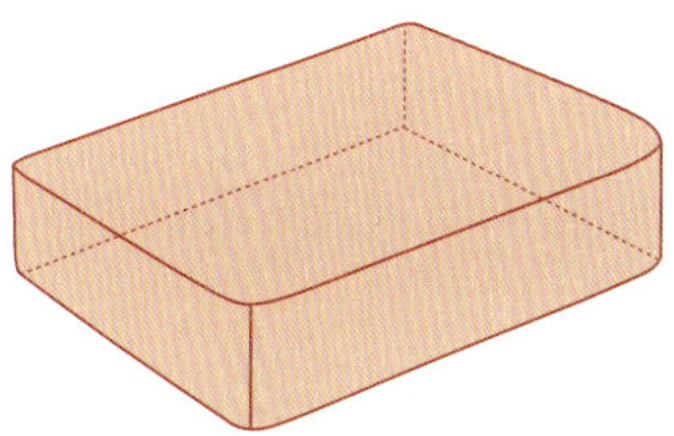

- Make cuts along the dotted-lines, fold the sides of the box and four corners of the paper accordingly, and apply the glue to the joints.

- Score the pattern to adorn the object.

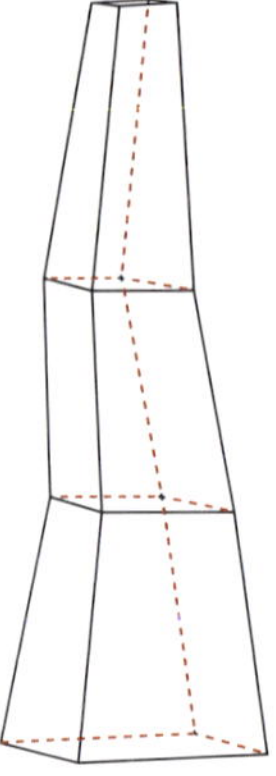

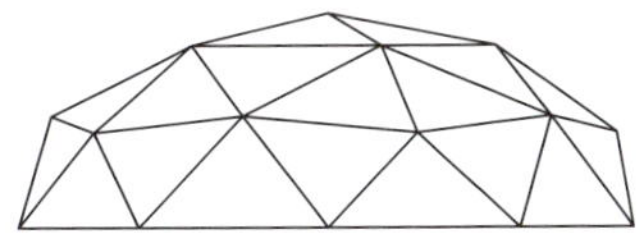

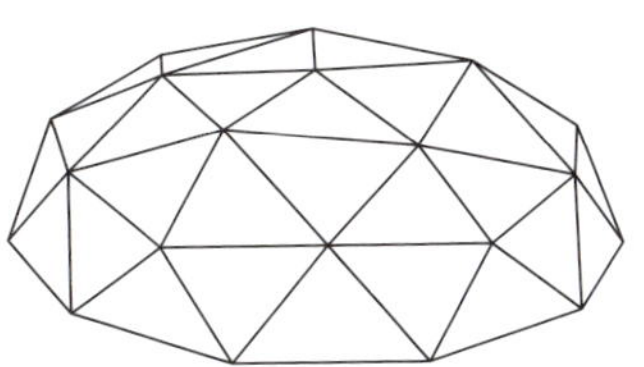

Illustration Guide Paris

Designer: Marina Delranc

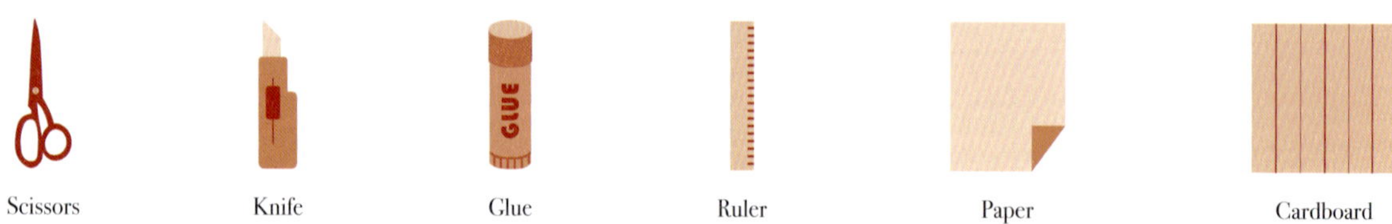

This work is an illustration in the guidebook *The Parisian cafes on Christmas*. The map showing the locations of cafes is presented in an unexpected way—attached to a knitted sweater. Inspired by Christmas window displays, the designer illustrated the Christmas theme with cutouts of stars, angels and trumpets. The image of a hot drink, echoing the topic of Parisian cafes, lures readers to start a cafe-searching journey.

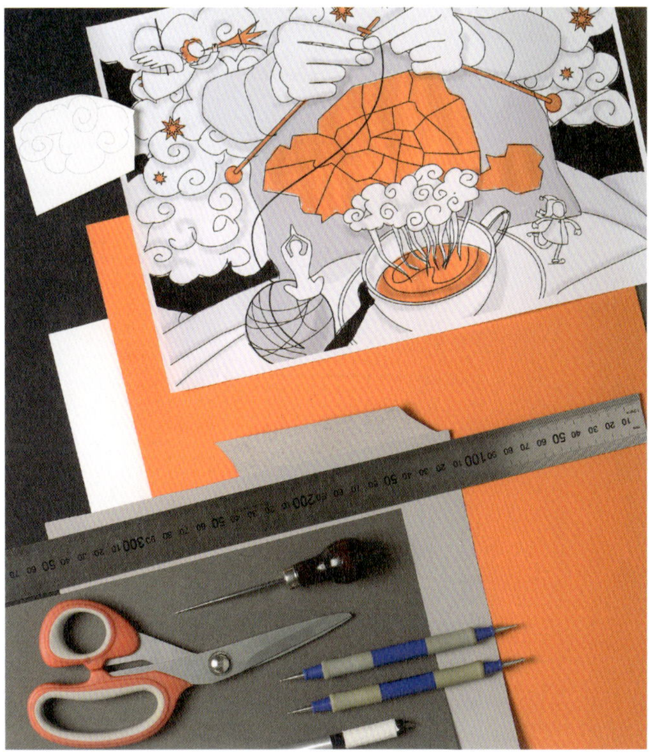

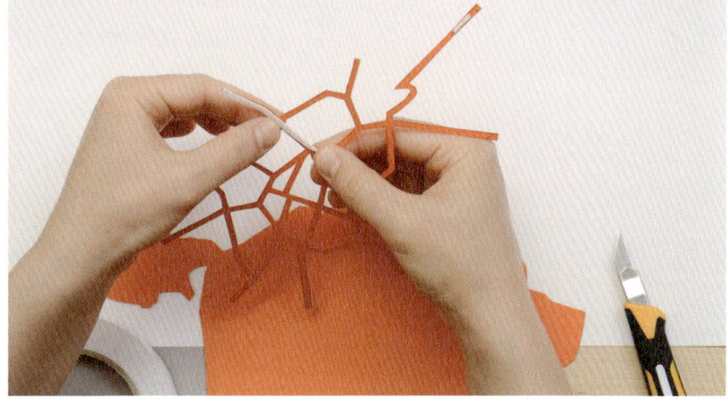

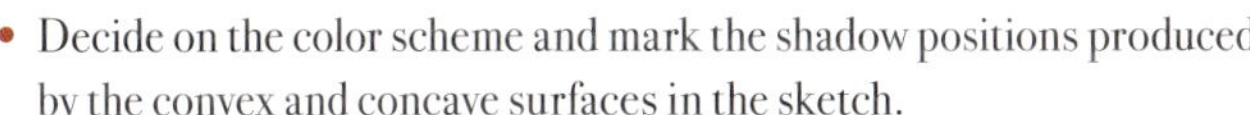

- Decide on the color scheme and mark the shadow positions produced by the convex and concave surfaces in the sketch.

- Make the cutouts and score the details on the paper. Put the adhesive strips on the back of every part and then connect one to another to construct the whole.

- Use an indentation pen to score the back of the paper. The outlines of the pattern will stand out and have a sense of depth.

- Work around the edges of each part with a stylus to create a 3-D curve.

Nissin Cup O' Noodles

Designer: Jeff Nishinaka

Pencil

French curve

Tweezer

Wooden dowel

Triangle

Paper [1]

A series of three posters were designed for a supermarket ad campaign for Cup O' Noodles. The campaign consists of three different promotional events: Winter Ware for the winter season, Holiday Souper Savor during the holidays and Scholarship prizes for students back to school.

[1] Strathmore Vellum Paper

Prior to cutting, decide on the lighting and the exposure angle.

Bend the edges to achieve a three-dimensional effect.

The mountain folds will be easier if you score them first with a knife.

Expoljuí-Fenadi Trade and Culture Fair

Designer: Carlos Meira

This paper sculpture was aimed at creating a promotional poster for Expojuí-Fenadi Trade and culture fair in the state of Rio Grande do Sul, Brazil.

[1] Paper (160 or 170g), watercolor paper (300g)

- Draw the draft and mark each colored part.

- Paint one side of the paper with watercolors and transfer the outline drawing on the other side by rubbing.

- Crease the paper down the center and bend the edges to deepen the crease. Be careful not to press down on the folded side of the paper.

Ural Psychoanalytic Bulletin

Designer: Anna Simonova

Ural psychoanalytic association

URAL PSYCHOANALYTIC BULLETIN

Proceedings of the international conference 2011-2017

Ekaterinburg
2018

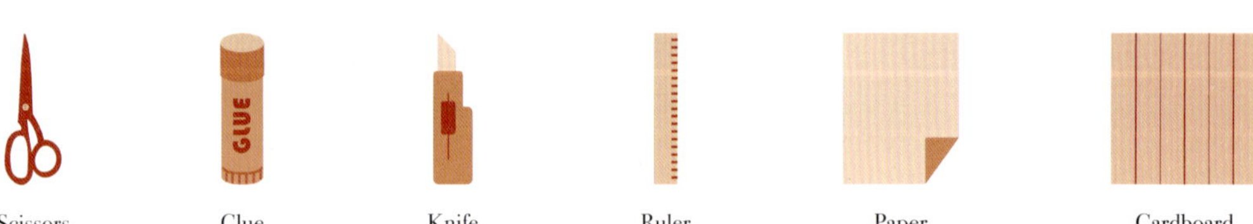

The cover of the book aims to incorporate the complexity and depth of human unconsciousness with layers of cut-out human profiles. Cutouts of stars, clouds, the sun, and the moon on the layers illustrate the idea of "a person as a micro-cosm," pairing with a universe outside the human body. The central tree representing the human brain connects the two universes.

- Make the sketch and mark the position of shadows between the layers.

- Cut out the figures and decide on the positions of every element.

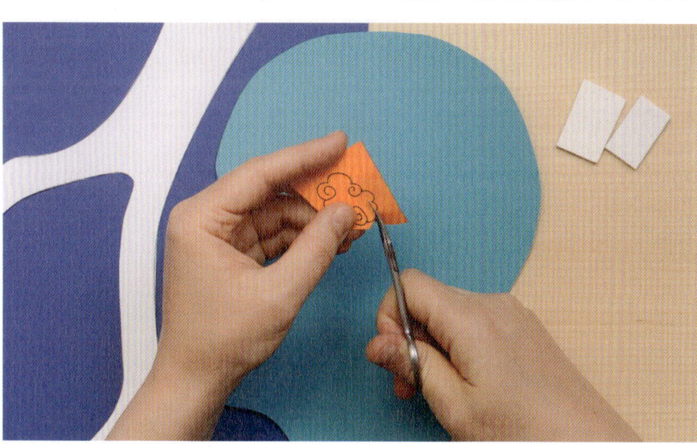

- Assemble the elements with glue or long transparent adhesive strips.

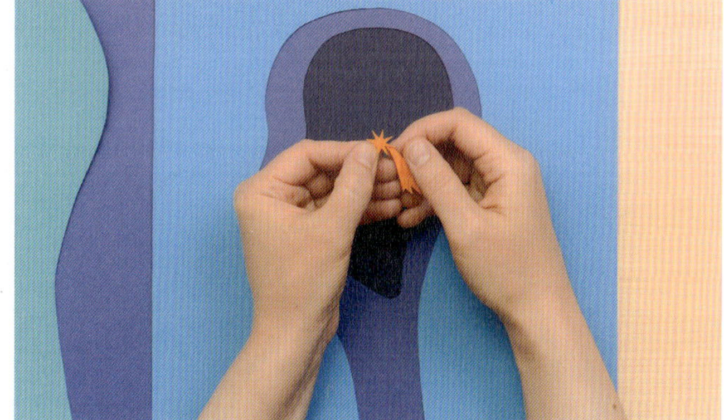

- Finish the hollowed-out parts with a knife.

London Socks Brand "Chatty Feet"

Designer: Yeni Kim

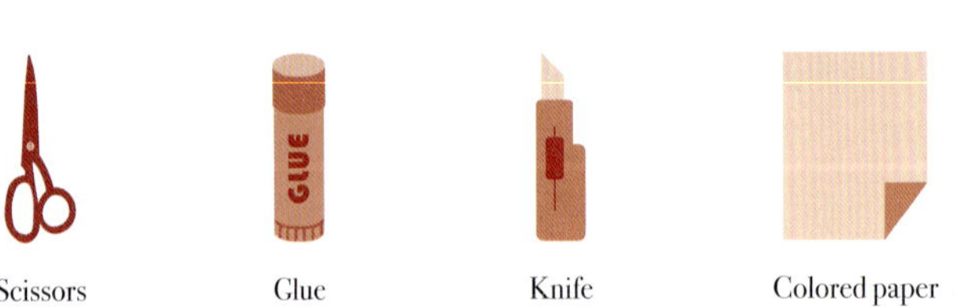

These three paper sets were designed and created by Yeni Kim for the London Socks Brand Chatty Feet. Receiving inspiration from the unique design of each pair of socks, the designer envisioned which objects should be included in the surroundings and how the socks could be made to look real. The project added humor and wit to the sets and created harmony among colors (Tone & Manner), making the socks appear naturally in the sets and to stand out.

My Amazing Body Machine

Designer: Owen Gildersleeve

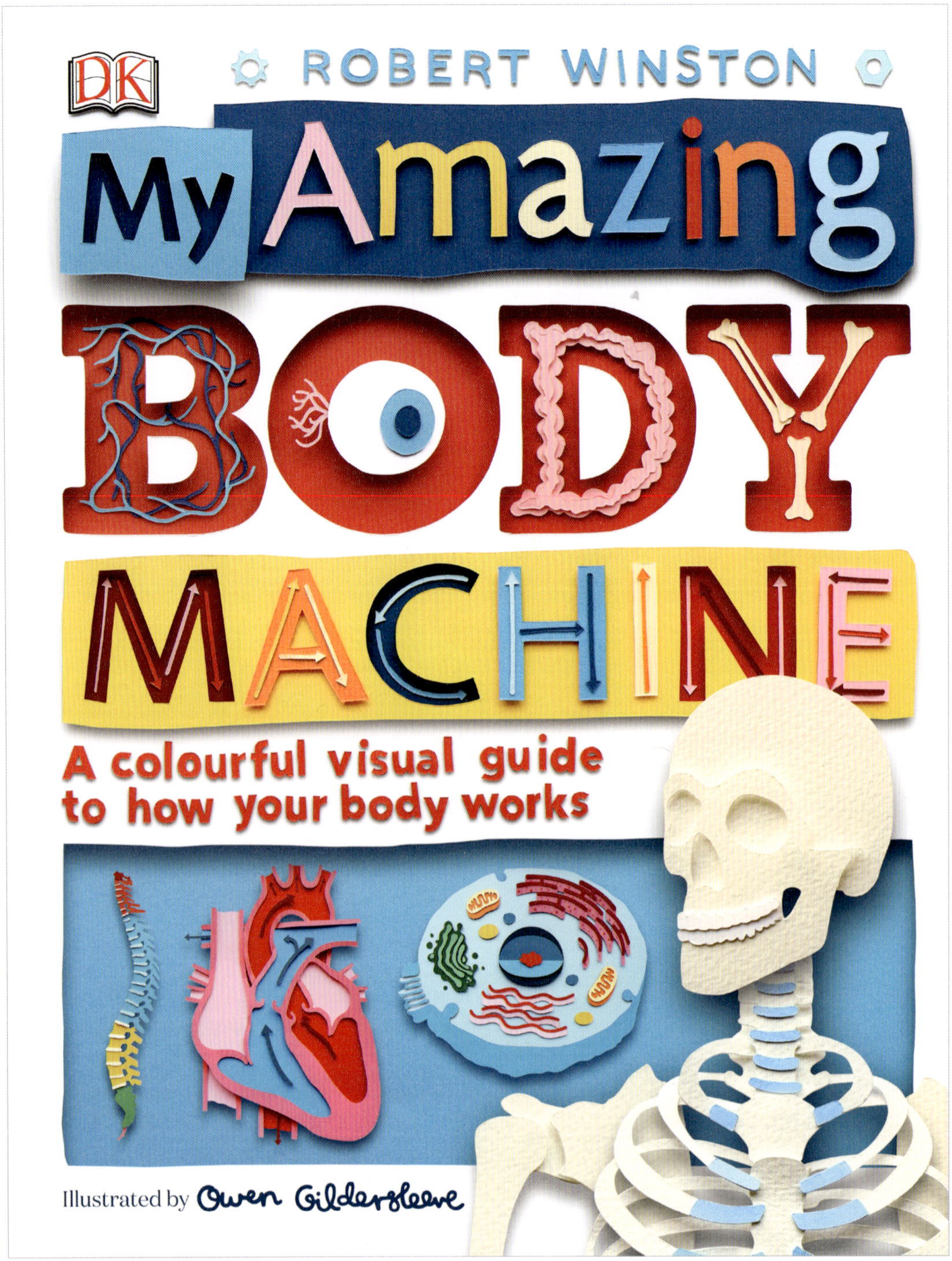

A series of fifty hand-cut artworks were created to illustrate the new book called *My Amazing Body Machine* by taking young readers on a unique and exciting journey through human anatomy. Bringing to life professor Robert Winston's explorations of the human body, the designer constructed intricate paper-craft artworks of all the working parts of human anatomy. He used layered paper and blocks of color to create the realistic diagrams, working with scientific consultants to ensure that each piece, from the intricately wired brain and nervous system to the framework of the skeleton, was anatomically correct.

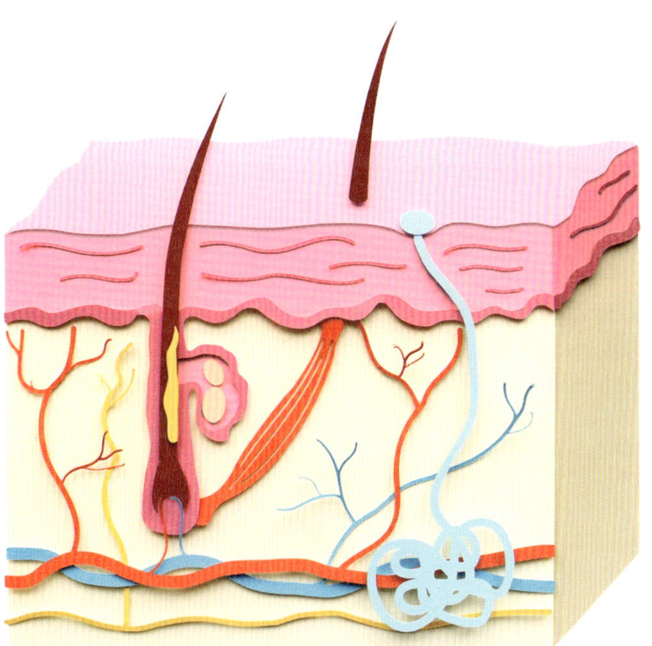

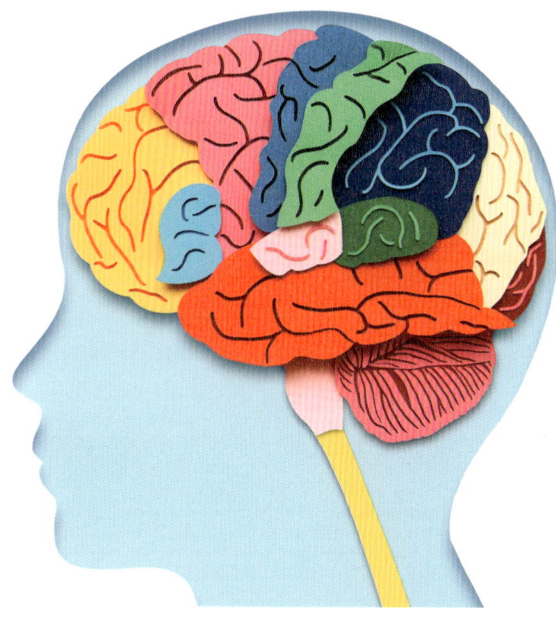

Seeing

Most of what you know about the world comes to you through your sense of sight. Your eyes pick up light from objects. They pass this information to your brain, so you can see the world around you.

How we see

Light rays enter your eye through a window called the cornea. The rays pass through a hole called the pupil and enter the lens. The lens changes shape to focus the light at the back of the eye, making an upside-down image. When signals from the eyes reach the brain, it creates an image that is the right way up.

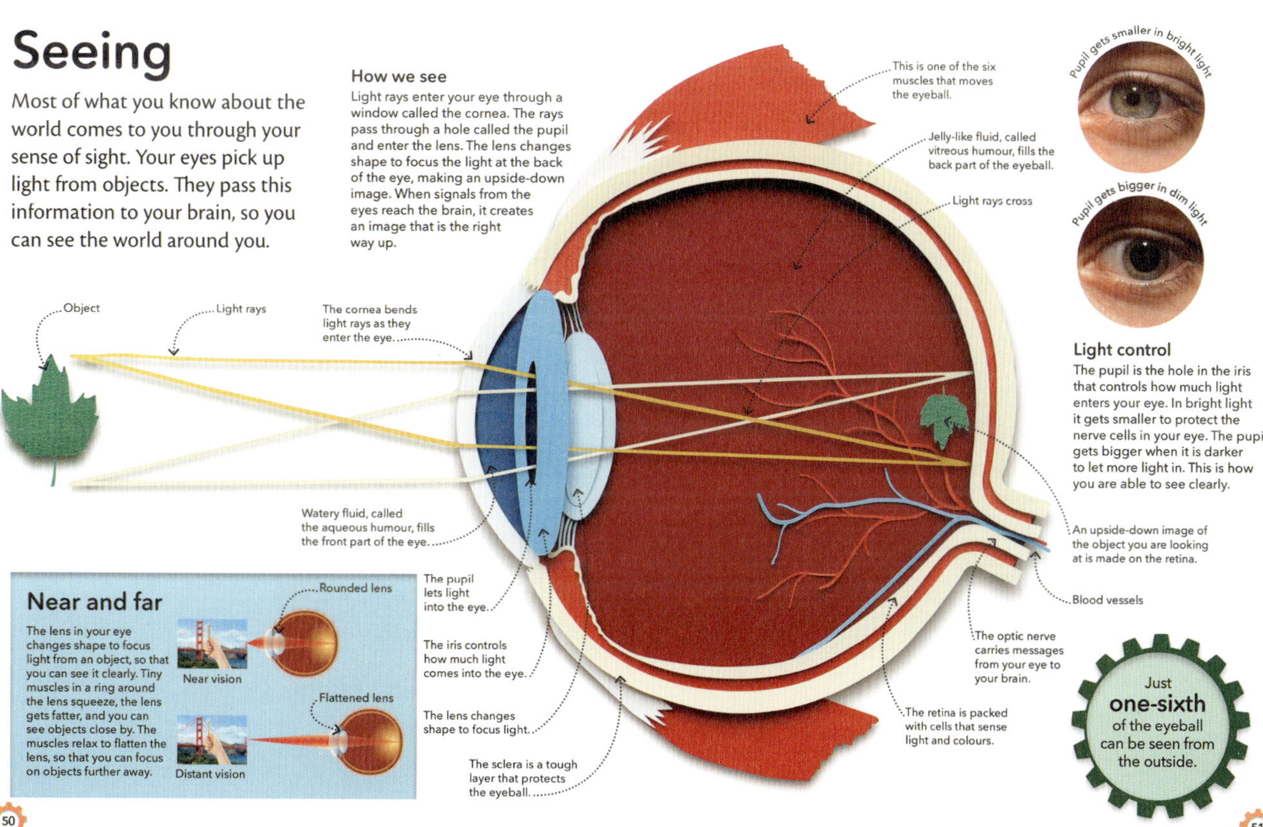

Light control

The pupil is the hole in the iris that controls how much light enters your eye. In bright light it gets smaller to protect the nerve cells in your eye. The pupil gets bigger when it is darker to let more light in. This is how you are able to see clearly.

Near and far

The lens in your eye changes shape to focus light from an object, so that you can see it clearly. Tiny muscles in a ring around the lens squeeze, the lens gets fatter, and you can see objects close by. The muscles relax to flatten the lens, so that you can focus on objects further away.

Moving machine

Whether walking, talking, or smiling, your body machine is constantly on the move. Muscles make those moves happen. Using fuel from food, muscles get shorter, or contract, to pull your bones. Other muscles pump your blood or help you eat and breathe.

Body muscles

The muscles that move your skeleton are found in layers under your skin. Here you can see surface muscles on the left and deeper muscles on the right. Some are named, along with the movements they produce. More than 640 skeletal muscles shape your body and make up half of your weight. Muscles are connected to your bones by tendons.

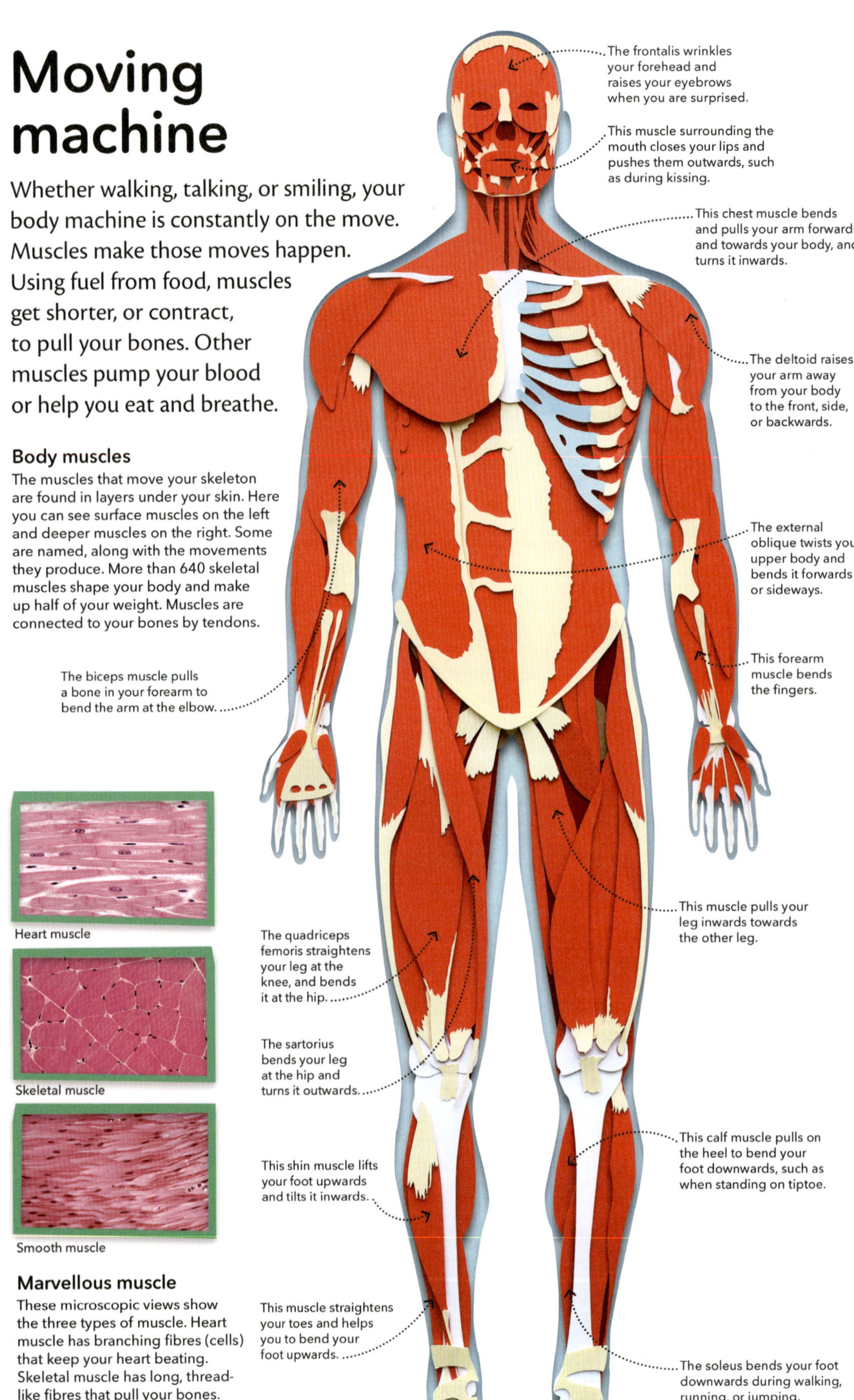

Heart muscle

Skeletal muscle

Smooth muscle

Marvellous muscle

These microscopic views show the three types of muscle. Heart muscle has branching fibres (cells) that keep your heart beating. Skeletal muscle has long, thread-like fibres that pull your bones. Smooth muscle squeezes hollow organs, such as your stomach.

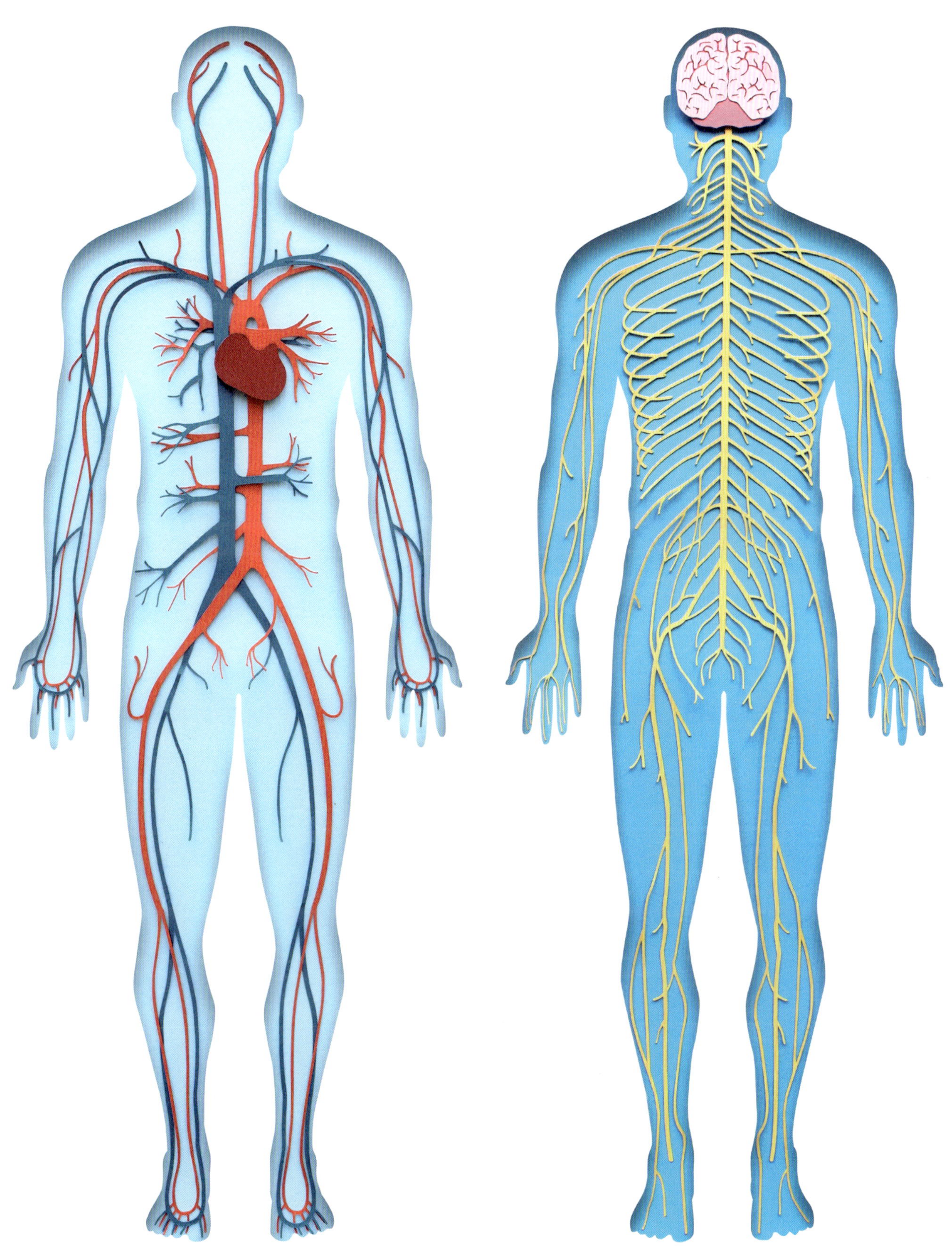

Anna Hu

Designer: Camille Ortoli

ANNA HU
HAUTE JOAILLERIE

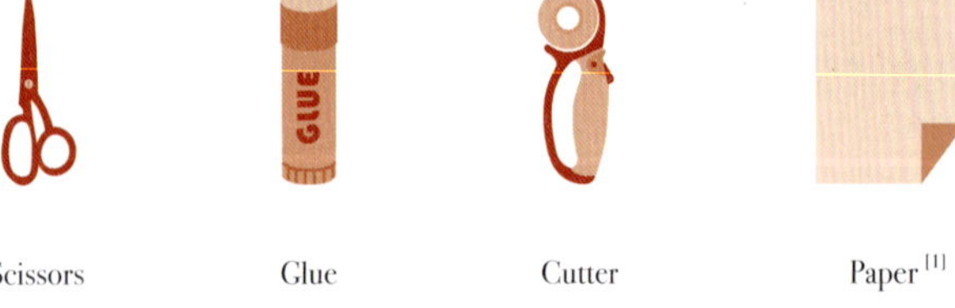

Scissors Glue Cutter Paper [1]

Inspired by landscapes and vegetation from Chinese paintings, the artist cut out fluid curved lines that suggest the contours of landscapes and rising mountains, as well as blooming flowers and vigorous leaves. In this case, the jewels are like treasures lying silently in Chinese nature. The pictures of the installations were featured in SOON Magazine.

[1] Canson paper

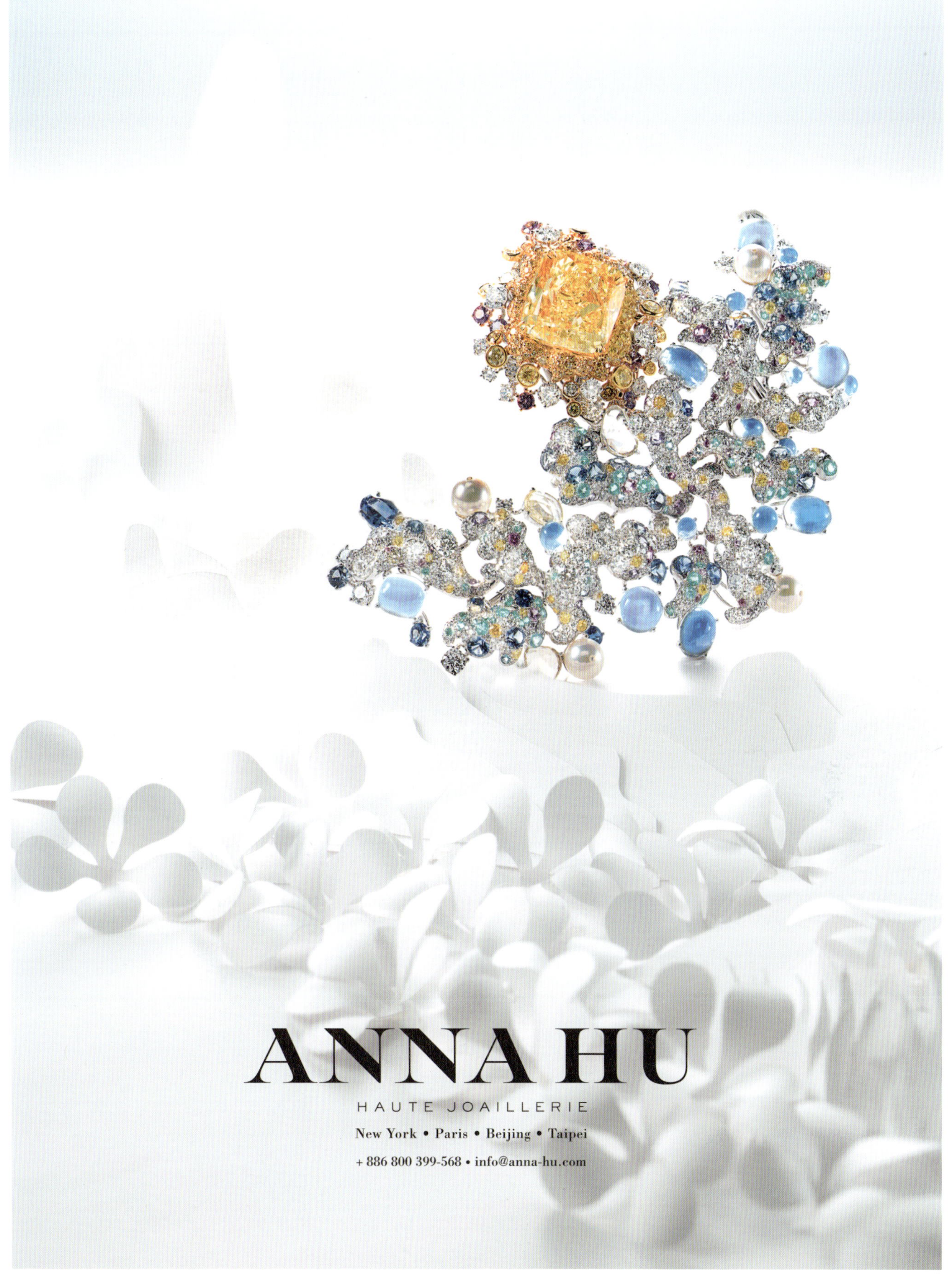
ANNA HU
HAUTE JOAILLERIE
New York • Paris • Beijing • Taipei
+ 886 800 399-568 • info@anna-hu.com

ANNA HU
HAUTE JOAILLERIE

ANNA HU
HAUTE JOAILLERIE

Scissors

Paper [1]

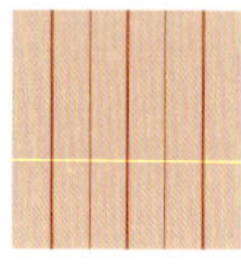

Cardboard

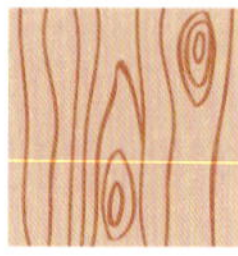

Wood

Displays in the windows of the prestigious luxury house of Hermès's flagship store in Charles de Gaulle airport in Paris, featured the theme of "The Meanwhile." The bright colors of the windows' palette was inspired by Hermès's iconic silk squares. The laundry represented the process of transformation and enhancement of the materials dear to the brand of Hermès. The office symbolized the design work, next to a room that showcased the products in their daily use.

[1] Canson paper

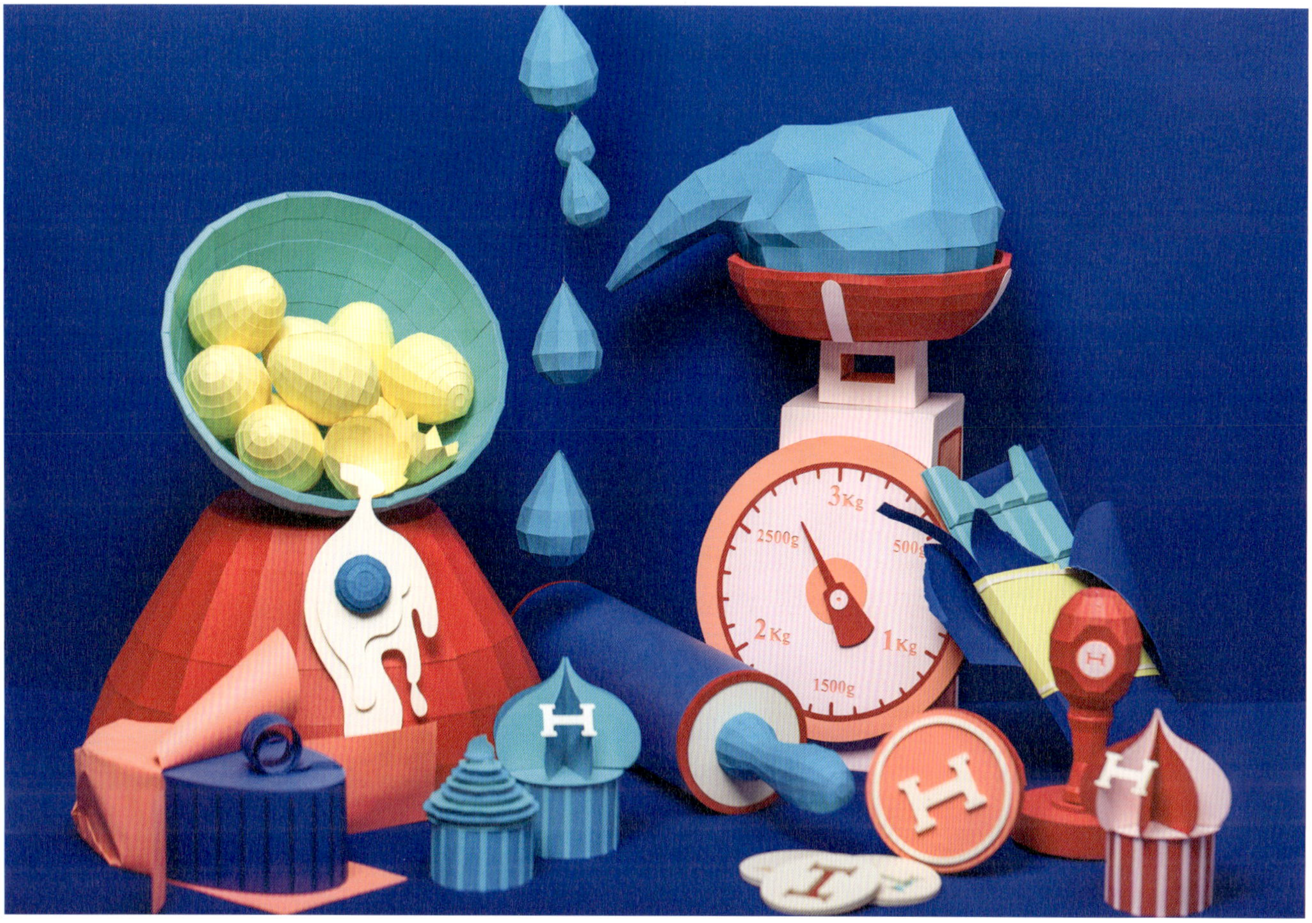
3Kg
2500g
500g
2Kg
1Kg
1500g

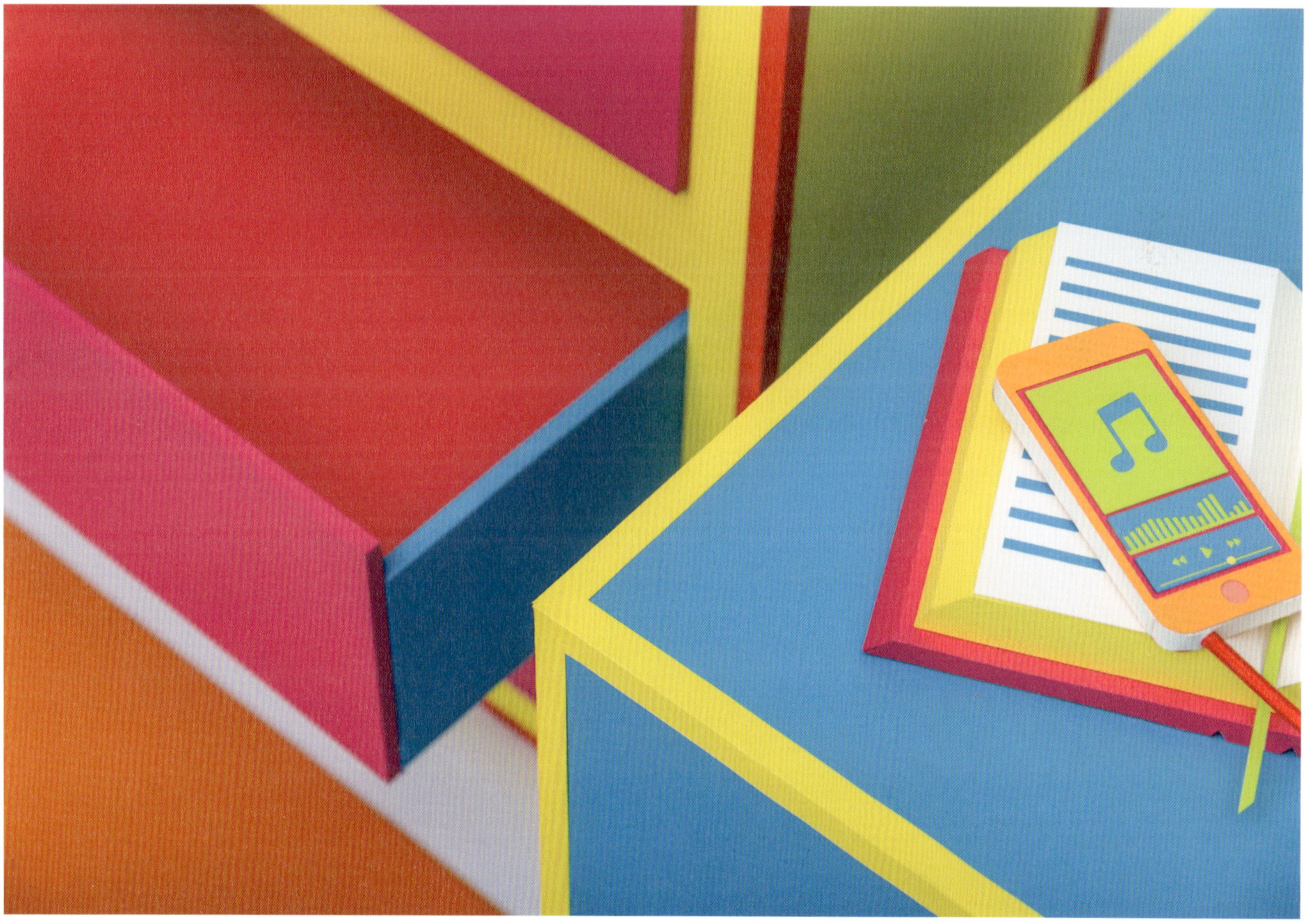

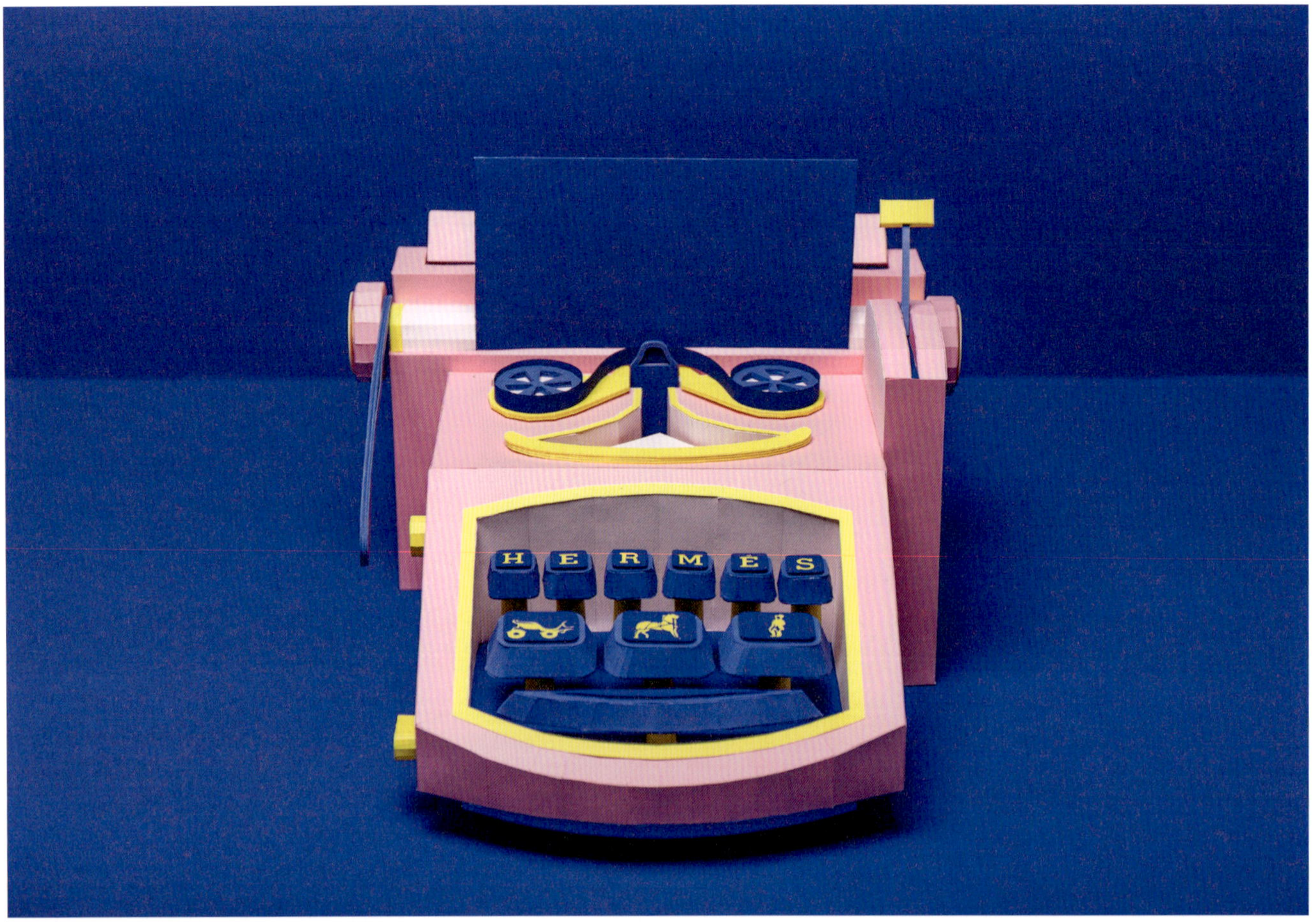

JACQUES CARELMAN
CATALOGUE OF IMPOSSIBLE OBJECTS
HERMÈS 2017
THE MEANING WHILE
PAPER DESIGN
ALINE HD

GLÜCKSBOTEN

Eine kleine Geste im richtigen Augenblick,
und in diesen Stücken funkelt das Leben. Für nachts,
für tags, für immer.

FOTOS INÈS DIELEMAN

Paper tape

X-acto blades

Scissors

Tweezers

Paper [1]

Inès Dieleman and Ollanski teamed up to show two series of of jewelry for the Christmas/Winter 2017 issues of KaDeWe magazine and ALSTERHAUS magazine, under the title Glücksboten, German for bearer of good tidings. With the winter theme, the project combined an all-white appearance with delicate, lovely, and playful details showing both plants and animals covered in ice and snow, to make the sparkling jewelry stand out like a star.

[1] Canson Velin's Mi-Teintes (white)

TIFFANY & CO.
Anhänger aus der Linie »Tiffany Enchant« und Halskette 12.900 und 550 Euro

WELLENDORFF
Ring »Brillant-Julia« 8.300 Euro,
Ring »Lebensglück« 12.700 Euro,
Ring »Sonnenglut« 12.900 Euro

79

OMEGA
Armreif aus der Linie »Ladymatic« 4.900 Euro

82

TIFFANY & CO.
Perlenhalskette aus der Linie »Ziegfeld« 1.450 Euro

CHOPARD
Ring aus der Linie »Copacabana« Preis auf Anfrage

BVLGARI
Ring aus der Linie »Serpenti« 8.980 Euro

Designer: Carlos Meira

The designer was invited to create a series of four covers of books for SAS based on the concepts: discover, explore, transform, and create. All the sculptures were created with colored papers and papers previously painted with watercolor and gouache.

[1] Paper (160 or 170g), Watercolor paper (300g)

CARLOS
MEIRA

BEA campaign

Designer: Nuttorn Vongsurawat

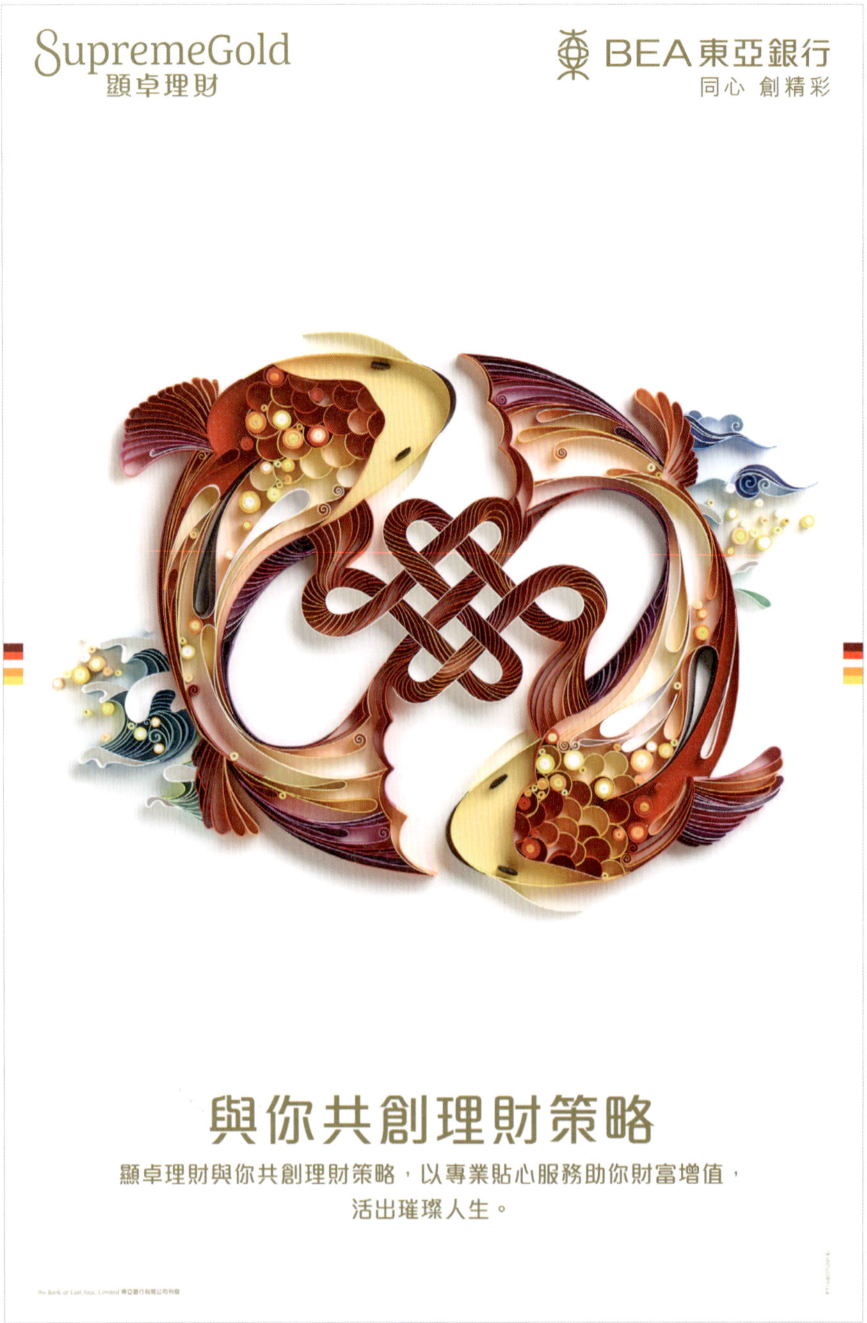

SupremeGold
顯卓理財

BEA東亞銀行
同心 創精彩

與你共創理財策略

顯卓理財與你共創理財策略，以專業貼心服務助你財富增值，
活出璀璨人生。

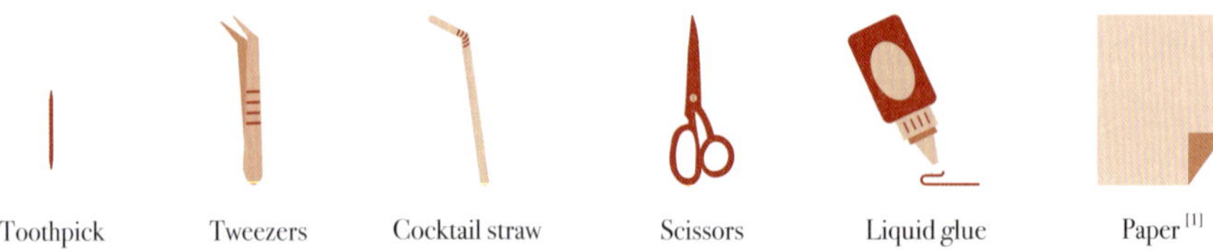

This is a premium banking advertising campaign for The Bank of East Asia (BEA), one of the largest licensed banks in Hong Kong. The project consisted of three unique paper illustrations applied horizontally on billboards, vertically on large lightbox posters and vertical billboards, as well as press ads. The first paper illustration depicted two swimming carp, joined by a Chinese knot, meaning to co-create your wealth together; the second paper illustration was composed of peony and bamboo, meaning to grow your wealth substantially; the third paper illustration showed a peacock with an open tail, meaning to make your wealth blossom.

[1] Heavy coloured paper, Card (around 200~300g)

Opéra Garnier

Designer: Marianne Guély

Iron wire Glue Paper [1]

This project consisted of paper decor for a private event at the Opera Garnier. The monumental decor displayed on the opera staircase was designed in collaboration with Potel & Chabot, a renowned Parisian caterer and events organizer.

[1] Non-woven coloured papers tinted by hand

ATRE
CHESTRE

Greco Roman Rainbow Pop

Studio: Anna-Wili Highfield

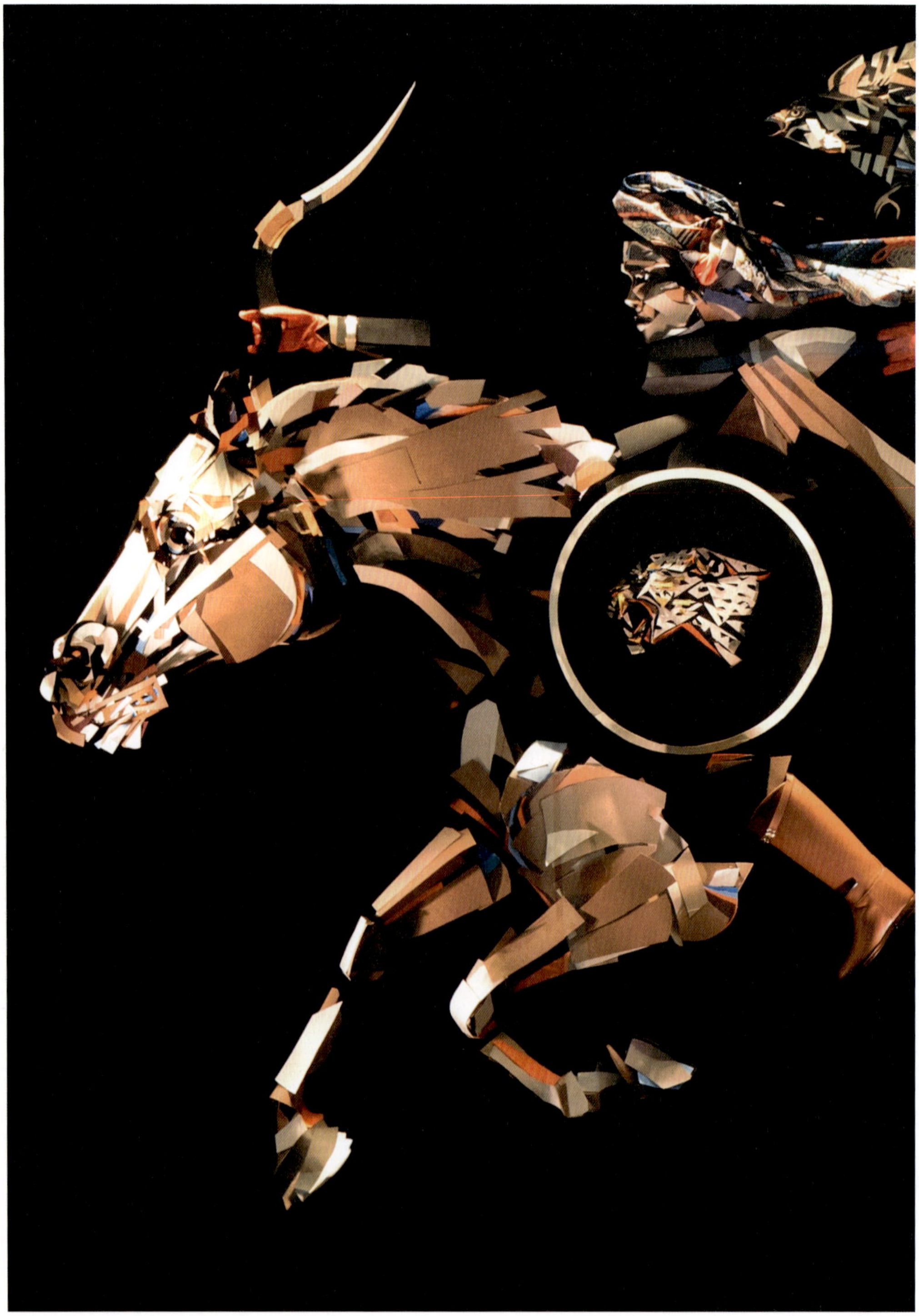

The inspiration for this project for Hermès came from Etruscan vases. The goal was to create a three-dimensional scene in paper that is dynamic and figurative, reminiscent of classical imagery from the ancient world. The use of colored paper for this project gives it a contemporary feel. Hermès products were used as sculptural elements in the piece as well.

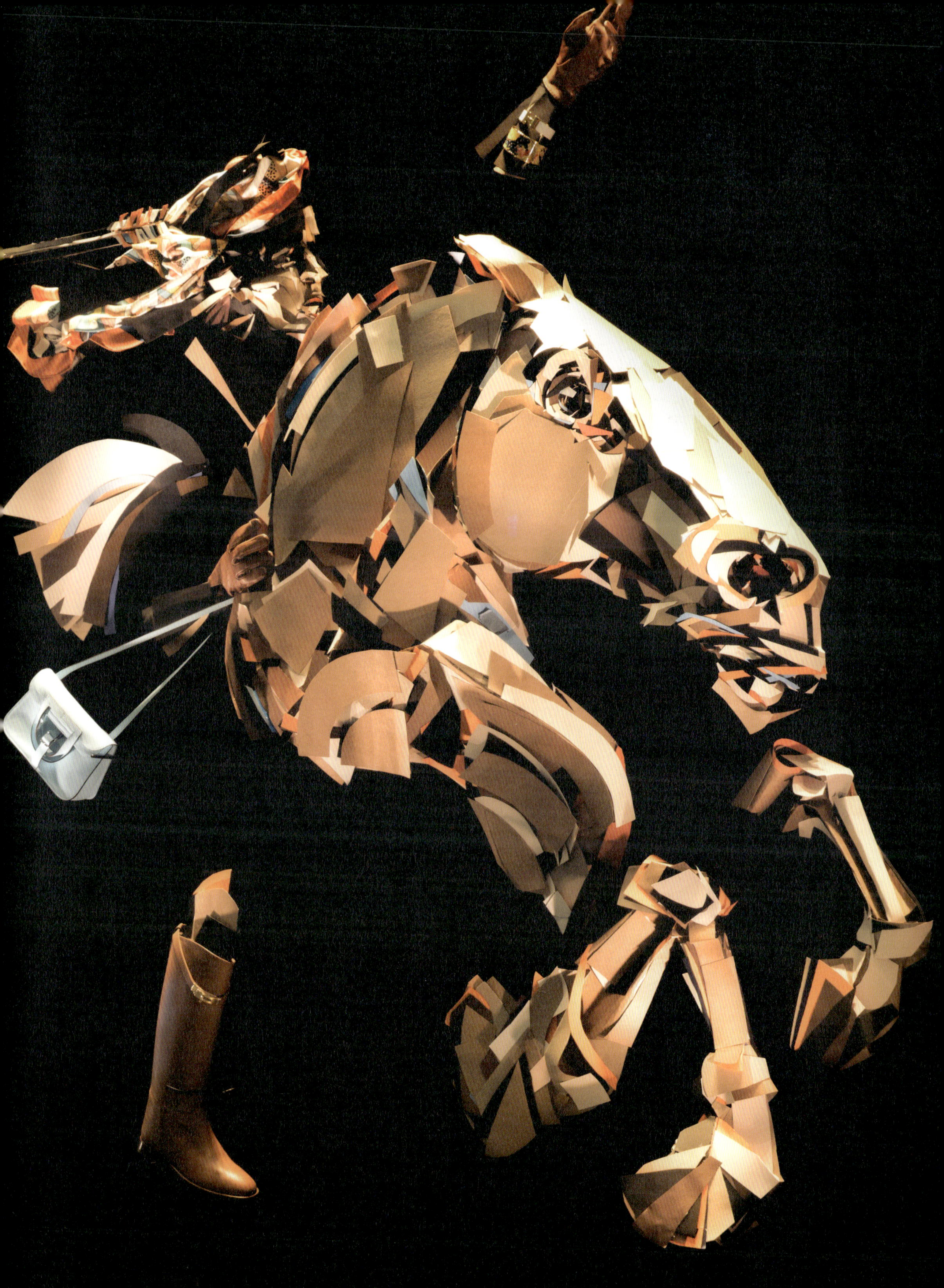

Natori New York Fashion Week

Designer: Antonius-Tin Bui

These projects were designed for a number of window displays for Josie Natori's New York storefront over the course of several years. The carving of the paper tapestries was directly influenced by the motifs, silhouettes, and textures presented in each season's look-book. These hand-cut window displays not only honor the respective collections, but highlight the architecture of the storefront as well. The shared passions for ornamentation and Asian American/Pacific Islander representation have led to fruitful collaborations.

[1] Hand-cut window displays, Drawing paper

Erin Peachee Lookbook

Designer: Julie Wilkinson

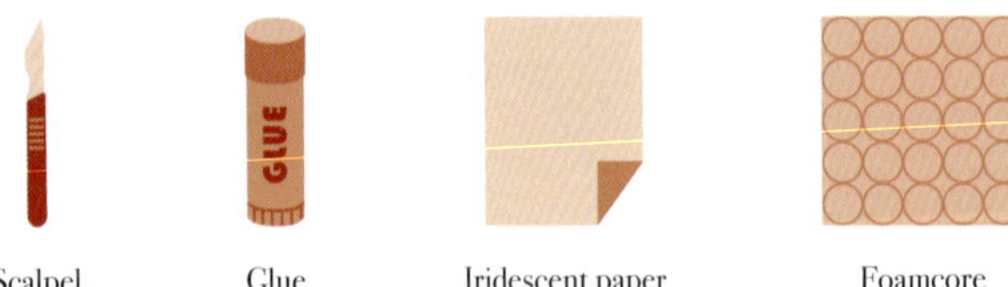

Scalpel Glue Iridescent paper Foamcore

The Erin Peachee lookbook was created for the launch of Erin Peachee's jewelry label. The designers created a set of New York building facades to complement the bold, and art deco-inspired lines of the collection and to showcase Erin's works in a striking way. The city buildings were constructed solely of black and white paper to to give the design a graphic look and added dimension. The jewelry was displayed on a number of painted hands moving in and out of the building windows, surrealistically symbolizing New York's inhabitants and their different personalities.

ERIN PEACHEE

Nestle — Love to Share

Designer: Gail Armstrong

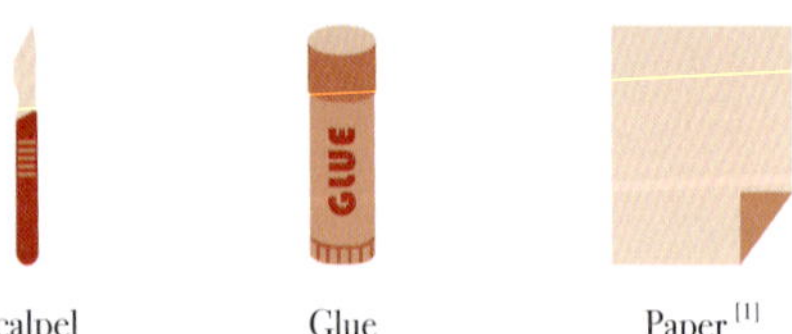

Scalpel Glue Paper [1]

Nestle–Love to Share, a paper-sculpture ad campaign that appeared largely in cinemas and points of sale, was created to promote Nestle's line of large bags of candy for sharing. Building on the graphic device of a lifted corner to reveal the Nestle logo, the project successfully created a paper world that highlighted the various ways and places the candy can be shared.

[1] Cartridge paper, Canson's Mi-Teintes, Daler Rowney's Murano and Conford, Winsor & Newton's Universal Coloured Paper (around 140~300g)

the clash
LOVE TO SHARE
Munchies
EXIT
Nestlé
Good Food, Good Life
Enjoy Nestlé Sharing Bags
Love to share

the double grab
No artificial colours, flavours or preservatives
Contains 25% fruit juice
Rowntrees
Fruit Pastilles

the red rummager
No artificial colours, flavours or preservatives
Contains 20% fruit juice
Rowntree's
Randoms

Kenali Nusantara

Designer: Ritter Willy Putra

Scissors

Paper [1]

Kenali Nusantara is a social initiative to engage young people living in village areas of Indonesia to learn and understand more about their country. The hidden wisdom of the project is the treasure behind every local scene, culture, and activity. The approach is warm and soothing, yet encouraging, which is intended to bring the audience a sense of emotional immersion in the messages.

[1] Manually crafted paper

akur
baur
makmur
kenali
nusantara
merantau
mengenal
Indonesia
sebuah program dari
Sabang Merauke
untuk informasi lebih lanjut,
kunjungi kenalinusantara.org
Temukan arti
di balik tradisi.
Yuk #merantaukedesa dan temukan hal-hal baru yang dapat menginspirasimu. Membayangkan saja tidak cukup, kamu harus mengalami dan merasakannya!

kenali
nusantara
merantau
mengenal
Indonesia
Temukan makna
di balik tawa.
Yuk #merantaukedesa dan temukan hal-hal baru yang dapat menginspirasimu. Membayangkan saja tidak cukup, kamu harus mengalami dan merasakannya!
sebuah program dari
SabangMerauke
untuk informasi lebih lanjut,
kunjungi kenalinusantara.org

kenali
nusantara
merantau
mengenal
Indonesia
sebuah program dari
SabangMerauke
untuk informasi lebih lanjut,
kunjungi kenalinusantara.org
Temukan teladan
di balik permainan.
Yuk #merantaukedesa dan temukan hal-hal baru
yang dapat menginspirasimu. Membayangkan
saja tidak cukup, kamu harus mengalami dan
merasakannya!

GNB Dental Calendar

Designer: Myeong-sook Joo

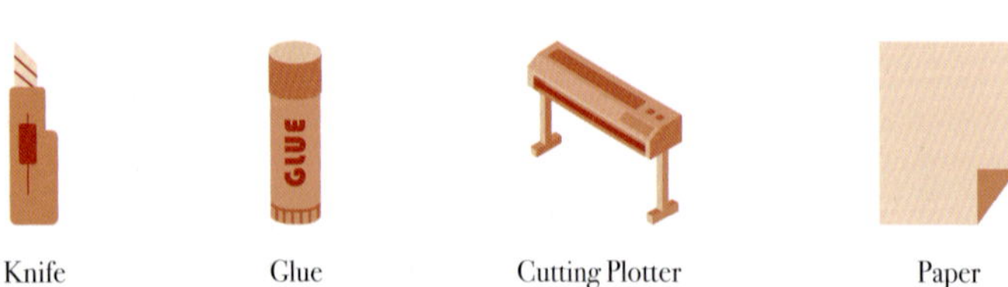

Knife Glue Cutting Plotter Paper

The designer's challenge was to work with the concept of creating a happy land of dental health. It was important to establish the 3-D volume of teeth, using paper, for this project. The designer kept the subject light and fun by adding fancy gift boxes, tooth-shaped balloons, puffy clouds, and cute characters.

Yamato Gift Catalogues—Mistral

Designer: Hiroko Matsushita

This series of illustrations was created for the cover of a catalogue of a gift company. All of the images were developed from keywords related to gifts: delivery, opening, and good luck.

[1] Ton Papier

Dolly Girl by Anna Sui Winter Catalogue

Designer: Hiroko Matsushita

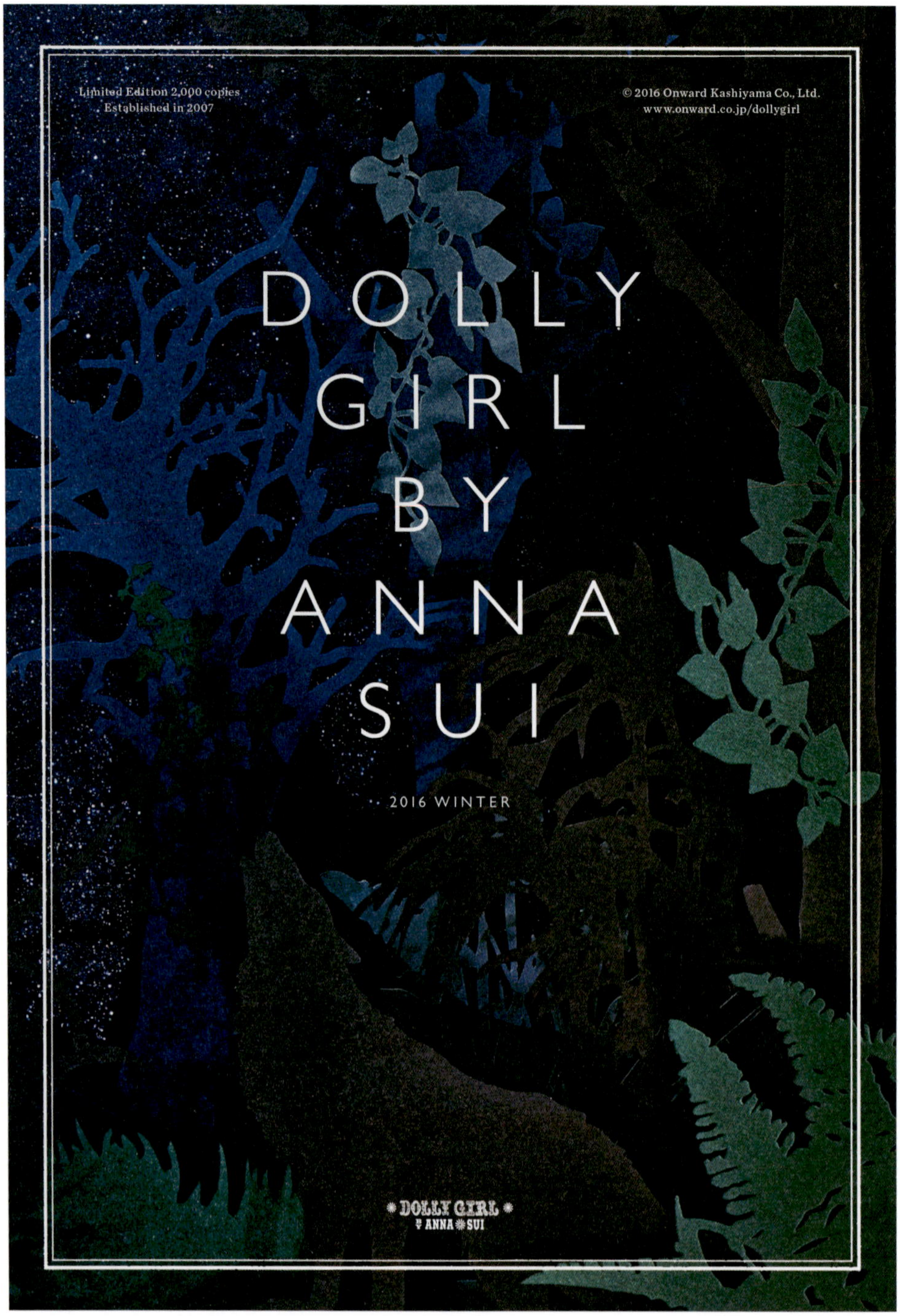

Limited Edition 2,000 copies
Established in 2007

© 2016 Onward Kashiyama Co., Ltd.
www.onward.co.jp/dollygirl

DOLLY GIRL BY ANNA SUI

2016 WINTER

DOLLY GIRL
ANNA SUI

X-acto blades | Cutting Plotter | Paper [1]

This project was a series of set designs for the fashion catalogue of a winter collection by Anna Sui. The concept for the collection—ballet—inspired the miniature theater sets, which were created with delicate paper art.

[1] Ton Papier

RUN AWAY, INTO
THE NIGHT FOREST

WONDERFUL TIMES
PASS BY IN A FLASH!

I WILL ALWAYS MEET
LOVELY NEW FRIENDS

THE UNKNOWN IS
ALWAYS SO EXCITING

Designer: Hiroko Matsushita

X-acto blades

Cutting Plotter

Paper [1]

A print advertising campaign was developed for the Japanese women's magazine, FRAU in collaboration with 6 cosmetic brands. Over 30 posters were displayed in Omotesandou station, one of Tokyo's major metro stations. The whimsical scenes were inspired by the city of Omotesandou to illustrate women's life in town, in nature, and at home.

[1] NT RASHA paper produced by Takeo, White drawing paper

Beauty Wonderland

SK-II

CELLUMINATION DAY SURGE UV

CELLUMINATION ESSENCE EX

FRaU

LIVING BEAUTY
暮らすだけでキレイになれたら!

FRaU
4月号 好評発売中 KODANSHA

SK-II
SK-II セルミネーション エッセンス EX
SK-II セルミネーション デイサージ UV (3月21日発売)
http://www.sk-ii.jp/

FRaU

FRaU
4

FRaU ORGANIC BEAUTY BOOK

LIVING BEAUTY
暮らすだけで
キレイになれたら!

Beauty Wonderland

FRaU
4月号 好評発売中

KODANSHA

Kleenex Feelings

Designer: Christiano Neves

Scalpel Glue Paper [1]

These illustrations were created for a Kleenex TV advertisement campaign with the catchphrase "Let It Out." In each illustration, a central figure was mirrored to show how Kleenex was there for both the good times and the bad, such as the positive and negative outcomes from a marriage, the glory and failure of a football player, the funny and sad moments experienced when reading.

[1] Cartridge paper, Canson's Mi-Teintes, Daler Rowney's Murano and Conford, Winsor & Newton's Universal Coloured Paper (around 140~300g)

IN
OUT
Tennis
TENNIS LESSONS
£10
£5
£1
666
000
000
666
STRESS
STRESS
STRESS
LOSER
COURT ORDER
Kleenex
Kleenex
Let it out
Let it out

IN
OUT
666
000
000
666
Kleenex
Kleenex
Let it out
Let it out

yum
Kleenex
let it out
yuk
FOOD £5
CLOSED
PLUMBER
JOBS
Kleenex
let it out
yum 
Kleenex
let it out
yuk
Kleenex
let it out

KING
No 1
TOUR
LET IT OUT
Kleenex
I U
SOLD
FOOL
TOUR

YES
LETITOUT
Kleenex

GLORY
LET IT OUT
Kleenex
10
CONTRACT
10
Kleenex
LET IT OUT
NEWS
REPOSSESSED
SOLD
FAILURE
WHISKY
FINAL REMINDER
DEBT

Designer: Laura Sayers

With the tagline "The home of thoughtful gifts," this miniature house—inspired by London townhouses at Christmas—was made and photographed for the cover of a magazine featuring handmade products from small businesses all over the world. Combining warm colors with playful scenes in each window, all on an incredibly small scale, this piece presents an idyllic Christmas scene.

[1] Paper by Colorplan, Maya, Canford with bronze details

HOUSE FOR NOTHS .

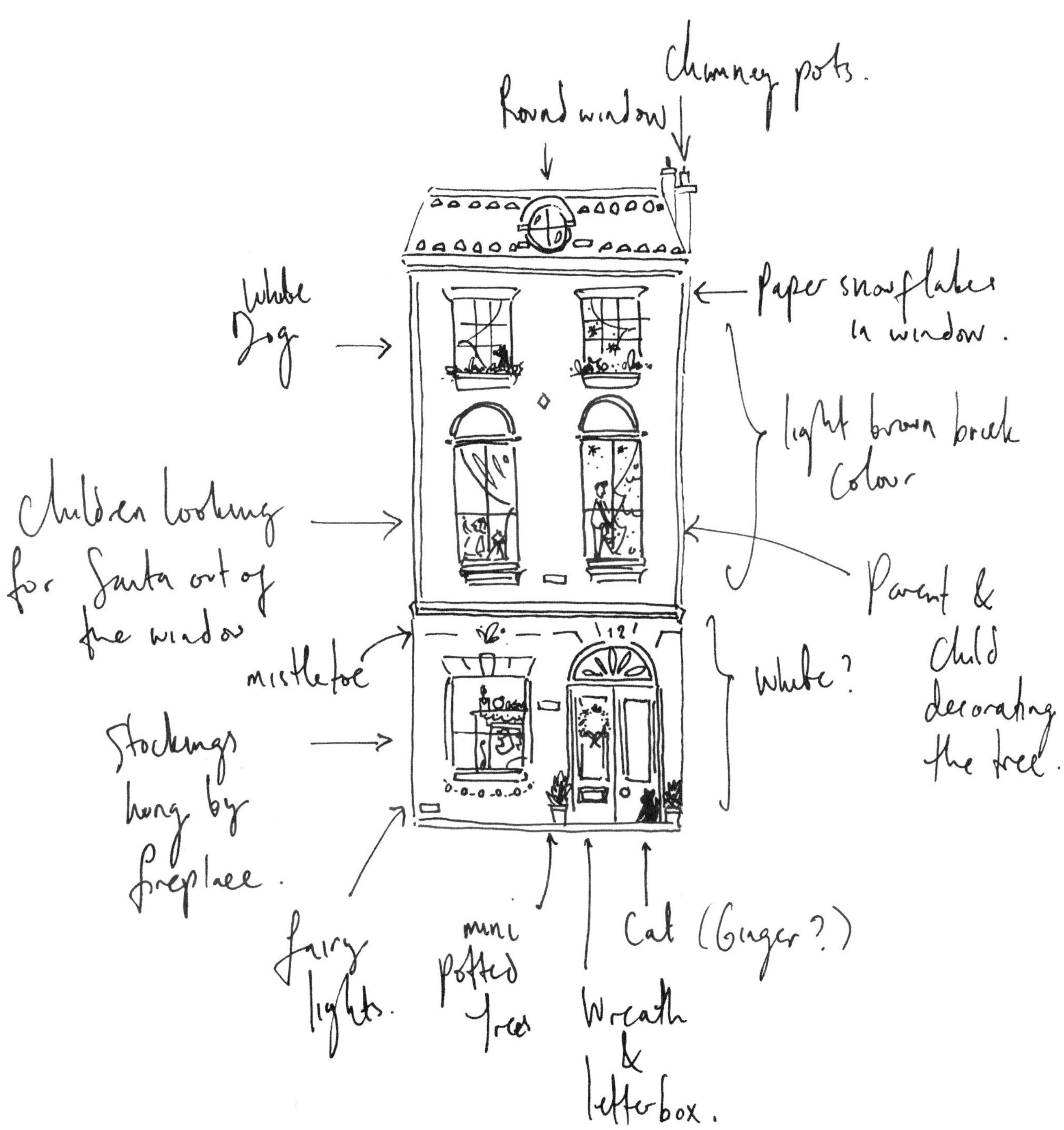

Viacom, Times Square New York

Designer: Tahiti Pehrson

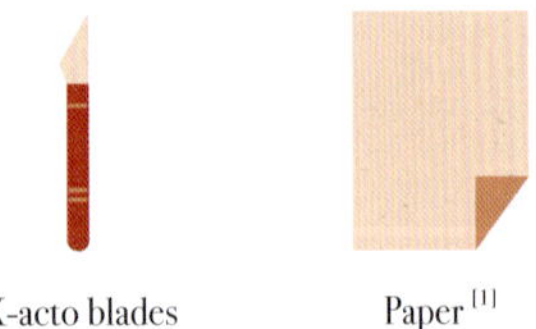

X-acto blades

Paper [1]

This project consisted of three installations symbolizing the three stages of life. The first stage–birth–was titled "The Fates" in a reference to Greek mythology. The installation was designed as three towers arranged as a three-dimensional triptych.

[1] Hand-cut 100% cotton rag paper, acid free

- The title of the second installation, symbolizing mid-life, was "Two Legs During the Day." The title was taken from The Riddle of the Sphinx in mythology, in which the phrase "walking on two legs" was a riddle for mid-life.

The last installation, The Transfiguration, is about Death or Rebirth. Moire patterns create movement as the viewer moves closer to the installation.

INDEX

ACKNOWLEDGEMENTS

We would like to thank all the designers and contributors who have been involved in the production of this book; their contributions have been indispensable to its creation. We would also like to express our gratitude to all the producers for their invaluable opinions and assistance throughout this project. And to the many others whose names are not credited but have made helpful suggestions, we thank you for your continuous support.

FUTURE PARTNERSHIPS:

If you wish to participate in SendPoints' future projects and publications, please send your website or portfolio to
editor01@sendpoints.cn.